THE DIGITAL SEEKER

THE
DIGITAL
SEEKER

A GUIDE FOR DIGITAL TEAMS TO
BUILD WINNING EXPERIENCES

RAJ K. DE DATTA

4 Columbia Business School
Publishing

Columbia University Press
Publishers Since 1893
New York   Chichester, West Sussex
cup.columbia.edu
Copyright © 2021 Bloomreach, Inc.
All rights reserved

Library of Congress Cataloging-in-Publication Data
Names: De Datta, Raj K., author.
Title: The digital seeker : a guide for digital teams to build winning experiences /
Raj K. De Datta.
Description: New York : Columbia University Press, [2021] | Includes index.
Identifiers: LCCN 2020055281 (print) | LCCN 2020055282 (ebook) |
ISBN 9780231202206 (hardback) | ISBN 9780231554442 (ebook)
Subjects: LCSH: Electronic commerce. | Consumer behavior.
Classification: LCC HF5548.32 .D397 2021 (print) | LCC HF5548.32 (ebook) |
DDC 658.8/72–dc23
LC record available at https://lccn.loc.gov/2020055281
LC ebook record available at https://lccn.loc.gov/2020055282

Columbia University Press books are printed on permanent and
durable acid-free paper.
Printed in the United States of America

Cover design: Noah Arlow
Cover image: Shutterstock

CONTENTS

INTRODUCTION

Embrace the Winning Formula

It wasn't always this complicated.

Twenty years ago you hired a couple of web developers and designers, bought them some pizza, and asked them to stand up a website. Those days were simple—the website was like a digital brochure. Most of the business was in the "real world," and the only expectation a customer had was for the website to represent whatever would have otherwise been in a physical brochure. We can call this the Brochure Age of the internet.

Then came Google and Facebook. A whole industry of marketers started running campaigns against those websites, and more and more people started arriving there. Your chief financial officer would then ask questions like "How do we make money on our website?" That led to a plethora of technologies and marketing tactics designed to build a digital business and to increase the probability that when a consumer or business came to your websites, and later apps, they would buy or sign up or engage or undertake whatever other action you wanted them to. Now we were spending real money. We were hiring armies of people to manually edit and curate those websites. We were spending millions of dollars on digital marketing. We can call this the Digital Marketing Age of the internet.

Pretty soon that digital marketing property became a core part of how we drove leads, customers, revenue, and service. It simply couldn't go down. It was performing a wide range of functions—service, sales, finance, supply chain, marketing, and so many others.

A parade of technology vendors arrived at your door, each promising a 20 percent revenue bump if you put their bit of tech on your website. Unfortunately, adding ten bits of technology didn't seem to increase revenue by 200 percent, and technology management became more and more challenging. How exactly do you figure out why your website is loading so slowly when you are dependent on ten external vendors and a bunch of external systems? Meanwhile, customers weren't just screaming about the problems—they were switching to native digital properties like Amazon, where billions of dollars of R&D assured a compelling digital experience. Their expectations had risen to where digital had become a utility, one that was expected to "always work." In fact, it didn't just need to work—it needed to delight them. We started to realize that the separation between the real world and the digital world no longer existed. They had become one and the same. We can call this the Digital Business Age of the internet. No longer are our digital properties just about marketing—they are the framework of the whole business.

In the Digital Business Age, your customers are getting restless. Options have proliferated, but somehow customers have been tasked with doing the work of sorting them all out. Think about the last time you tried doing holiday shopping online. Chances are you started with optimism, hitting the search engines and looking for great gifts. But after a frustrating period of clicking around, you likely defaulted to the Amazon best-sellers list just to get out of there. My company, Bloomreach, powers search and digital experiences for thousands of the largest brands on the planet, including 25 percent of e-commerce in the United States and the UK. Looking at our data set of billions of consumer interactions going back ten years, I can see us searching for content, products, and services. I can see our hopes and dreams playing out in trend lines and keywords. And I can see unfulfilled customers and failing digital experiences in the form of stagnant conversion rates, high bounce rates, and uninspired customer journeys. And then I can see them go to Amazon or some Silicon Valley upstart.

As this plays out, digital teams are wrestling with the challenges they see. Often they are the savants, charged with saving the company from looming disruption. They struggle with conflicting goals, a lack of resources, a talent gap, antiquated technology stacks, nimble competitors, and rising operational and financial targets. Something has got to give.

The practices we learned when the internet was all about marketing are failing us in the Digital Business Age. And our customers are paying the price for it. Classic internet experiences are not giving customers what they're seeking. Instead, they are turning our customers into screen-hogging automatons, sifting through the noise of the Web trying to find their way. They are turning our businesses into silos—the digital world versus the real world, with one struggling to compete with upstarts and the other continuing to fight yesterday's battles. They are frustrating our digital teams, which often know what to do but struggle profoundly to make the substantial shifts needed to drive progress more quickly.

All this frustration raises a very basic question about why we have the internet in our lives at all: Wasn't this whole internet thing supposed to make our lives simple and easy and straightforward? It doesn't seem to be working out quite that way.

But amid the frustration and the struggles, I see companies winning big across the hundreds of digital businesses we at Bloomreach serve, across my personal investments as an angel investor in tens of start-ups, and across the broader ecosystem of digital contenders. The winners aren't just the Silicon Valley success stories we all know—Google, Facebook, Apple, and Amazon. I see public-sector organizations like the National Health Service (NHS) in the UK innovating in health care delivery. I see fashion innovators like Stitch Fix and Rent the Runway remaking fashion. I see business-to-business (B2B) distributors like Watsco and MSC Direct reinventing their interactions with field technicians. I see local sports teams like Bayern Munich reimagining their relationships with fans worldwide. I see innovators like HotelTonight rethinking the travel industry by identifying a whole new need for spontaneous travel. And I see organizations like the United States Tennis Association leapfrogging other tennis powerhouses using the power of artificial intelligence (AI) and analytics. Each of these organizations falls into a distinct pattern that drives its winning.

I see that the winners in the Digital Business Age have three things in common:

- *Winning digital experiences are built for the seeker, not the customer.* They don't just enable customers to buy or find something; instead, they enable customers to find the solutions they are seeking for deeper problems.
- *Winning digital experiences are built on a digital experience platform (DXP).* They collect cutting-edge technology such as AI on a common platform that delivers agile, personalized, and scalable performance.
- *Winning digital experiences are built by product-centric digital teams with innovative new business models.* Every aspect of organization, culture, and operation follows the business model of a Silicon Valley software company rather than that of a traditional organization.

How all that happens is the stuff of this book. We'll profile a number of the winners, tracing their journeys and their conclusions. We'll distill the three key attributes needed to win big in digital and provide a road map for all digital teams to adopt them. Our structure for doing all this is as follows:

Chapter 1: Break Online/Offline Boundaries—The new age of digital is defined by the breaking of historical boundaries between the digital and the real worlds. To explain how we arrived in this new age, we'll tell the Cedar Fair transformation story. Cedar Fair operates the famous Cedar Point as well as Kings Island, Canada's Wonderland, Great America, and other amusement parks. It's possible to break internet history into three distinct periods, and Cedar Point is a perfect case in point. In this chapter, we'll explain why the new Digital Business Age is different from earlier ages in the evolution of the internet and what digital teams must embrace to create winning experiences today.

Chapter 2: Put the Seeker at the Center—Digital winners find the seekers behind their customers and build for them. We'll share the stories of Stitch Fix, NHS Digital, HotelTonight, Flyhomes, Bayern Munich, and Uncommon Goods.

Chapter 3: Swap Customers for Seekers—We'll explain what the difference is between customer and seeker and why understanding the distinction is the difference between winning big and becoming obsolete. Customer-centric initiatives typically involve looking at customer-facing functions (sales, customer service, etc.) and improving them. But they do not ask a fundamental question: Why does a customer want my product? Understanding underlying motivations often results in the realization that a customer has "a job to do" or "a task to complete." Seeker centricity involves really understanding these motivations and providing everything the customer needs to meet that goal. Winning digital means winning the seekers.

Chapter 4: Harness the Three As—We'll investigate the three As: AI, ambient technology, and application programming interfaces (APIs). These profoundly important technology trends have transformed digital experiences, enabling practitioners to build magical digital experiences that speak to the seeker. They provide the baseline technologies that form the core of a DXP, each one adding its own magic and together providing compounding benefits. We'll share the stories of DeepMind, Google, Kespry, and the United States Tennis Association.

Chapter 5: Build Your Digital Dreams; Don't Buy Them—We'll dive into the modern digital technology stack, which should form the basis of innovation for the future. The DXP is a new platform that harnesses the three As to transform digital experiences into engines for innovation, agility, and growth. We'll outline the key components of a DXP, with a particular focus on the commerce experience—tracing the evolution of early e-commerce stacks to the powerful platforms that winning businesses use to drive competitive advantage. We'll share the stories of commercetools and Blue Apron.

Chapter 6: Design for Disaster—We'll examine six of the core tenets of great digital experiences that scale: privacy, security, reliability, performance, explainability, and diversity. In the face of emerging regulatory restrictions, we'll explore how to leverage large data sets and AI in a DXP but still ensure that diversity is maximized and privacy is honored. We'll examine the core architectural principles that powerful technologies like APIs and ambient require from a modern DXP. We'll share the stories of IKEA and Bloomreach.

Chapter 7: Recast Your Team to Ship—Meet the new team. The digital team of the future will be product centric, not function centric. We'll see the emergence of a whole host of new leaders with titles like chief digital officer and teams with skills that had never made it into enterprises in the past, including product manager, designer, developer, and others. We'll see these teams operate within product-centric cultures, use agile development processes, and leverage lean methodologies to ship their products and iterate their way to digital success.

Chapter 8: Create Your Money-Making Architecture—We'll examine the business models of winning digital businesses, considering how they approach making money in very different ways. We'll investigate how these businesses invest over long horizons, market creatively, play on a different competitive playing field, mitigate risk, build ecosystems, and scale with greater leverage. We'll see that winning teams leave sunk costs behind, imagining their business plan the way a disruptor might. We'll share stories of Atlassian, Hobbycraft, Next plc, and Olo.

Chapter 9: The Winning B2B Experience—Winners are not remaking the internet as an exclusively consumer platform. While B2B experiences have a lot in common with consumer-facing experiences, they remain different in important ways. We'll dive into what's common and what's unique about B2B digital experiences, including the teams that build them, the metrics they optimize for, the motivations of their customers, and the technology implications. We'll share the stories of MSC Industrial Direct, Sandvik Coromant, Staples, and Watsco.

Chapter 10: Max Out the Ro—Even as we shift to this new Digital Business Age, the next shift is already brewing. We'll explore the post-COVID-19 digital world, tracing the accelerations the pandemic has created and the implications for digital practitioners and consumers. What are the issues for the future that this current digital age will bring us? How has COVID-19 changed our digital experience? Will it last? In particular, we'll discuss who will win in the long term and who will lose—challenging conventional wisdom that the digital behemoths of Facebook, Google, Amazon, Microsoft, and Apple are inevitable victors.

At the end of this road map lie treasures that benefit all the stakeholders of digital business—teams, businesses, and consumers. For teams, treasure means high-velocity innovation around deep and transformative customer solutions that lead to leadership and career advancement. For businesses, it means a high degree of competitive advantage grounded in unique offerings that lead to outsized profits. For consumers, it means a world where the right collection of products, services, and experiences comes to you, so that you spend less time on your digital to-do list and more time on the things you love doing. Think of it like Iron Man's armored suit that snaps on when he's in motion—just in time to fight the enemy.

Let's get to the winning.

Winning digital experiences are built for seekers.

Winning digital experiences are built on a digital experience platform.

Winning digital experiences are built by product-centric teams.

Figure Intro.1 The three core principles of a winning digital experience.

THE DIGITAL SEEKER

1

BREAK ONLINE/OFFLINE BOUNDARIES

If your summer plans have ever taken you through Ohio, then you've seen them. They fill the highways and roadside diner parking lots. The minivans and station wagons—the family cars packed with family members and often with a unifying soap crayon message scrawled on the back window: Cedar Point, Here We Come!

Cedar Point is no ordinary amusement park. The 364-acre complex jutting into Lake Erie is a midwestern tradition. Operating continuously since 1870, it is the proud home of eighteen rollercoasters, including Millennium Force, the GateKeeper, and Steel Vengeance. While it started as a single park, it now also serves as the headquarters of Cedar Fair, a billion-dollar holding company for fifteen parks across the country that boasts stomach drops and shrieks among its quarterly goals.

Cedar has provided vacation fun for generations. And now it adds a new achievement to its resume: leader in the digital business revolution.

A company focused on old-time family outings may seem an odd place for a technology paradigm shift. But this is where we'll stop for a moment to demonstrate the enormity of what has already happened in the short life of the internet—and what is happening again, right now.

Figure 1.1 In the late nineteenth century, Cedar Point emerged as a popular vacation spot. Wikimedia Commons.

Figure 1.2 Cedar Point continues to thrill vacationers. Shutterstock.

It's possible to break internet history into three distinct periods, and Cedar Point is a perfect case in point.

Parent company Cedar Fair, like many legacy operations, did not hurry to leap onto the internet. There was nothing virtual about the business it was in. In the dot-com era, while everyone seemed to be chasing eyeballs and stock options, Cedar Fair was building the death-drop Power Tower and the Woodstock Express kiddie coaster. It kept focus on the real work of the real world, dipping into the virtual one only as necessary.

As with many companies, Cedar Fair's first foray online was a website. There was nothing complex about it. The site served as a basic billboard for the work of Cedar Fair—listing information about the parks such as hours, rides, ticket prices, and events. The corporate section featured financial data, executive bios, and press releases. It was essentially a virtual brochure, with a sprinkling of annual report. And it was what most brick-and-mortar companies were doing at the time: getting onto the internet because everyone was doing it. But the real action of the company was live—in the parks. Everybody knew that.

That was the first era of the internet. Let's call it the Brochure Age. Given what we do now, it seems quaint. But it was a big step for a firm that lived for the family road trip.

The plates shifted between 2005 and 2010 with the rise of Google and Facebook and the advertising opportunities they brought with them. These firms opened a new way to reach customers online. Instead of trying to attract customers to your quaint little website, you could now use Google and Facebook to find them wherever they were online. Digital billboards gave way to digital ad campaigns, reaching customers as they flowed into online entertainment and social media and the ever-expanding digital native experiences. Now firms didn't have to wait for customers. Instead, they could go out and find them. And they did—in spectacular numbers. The opportunities offered by Google and Facebook made first-gen websites look like cave drawings. Cedar Fair made the transition by charging its ad agency with managing its online advertising campaign. But its focus on the parks continued. The parks were where the magic happened. Cars still packed the parking lot with families. The job of the internet efforts was to get people to the website (and later the app) to attract them to the park. They came by the millions for real-world fun.

As we emerged from the economic downturn of 2008–2009, something new began to bubble up in the business world. By 2015, Cedar Fair execs saw it clearly: customers looked at the company website, and they clicked on the virtual ads—but that was not the end of their internet experience. They arrived in the parks bringing the internet with them. Mobile devices allowed them to carry it in their hands and purses and fanny packs. Now the experience of Cedar Point included this new, uninvited guest. Park goers melded rides and water parks with texting and social media. A freshly made funnel cake's first stop was likely Instagram. Vacation photos went straight to Facebook. Decisions about dinner were filtered through handheld search engines and vetted through Yelp reviews. Park goers brought more than their devices and habits to the park—they also brought the demands born of their experience. Now exposed to innovative companies such as Uber, Spotify, and Apple, they looked for that same level of experience in their favorite vacation.

It was an evolution driven by customers, recalls Jim Denny, vice president of e-commerce for Cedar Fair. "The customer twisted everything on us; the whole model is different," he says. Families in Cedar Fair parks had taken mobile and social media into their lives. "That changed the entire world, and the question we had to ask ourselves was 'Do we fit into that world?' "

Not in Cedar Fair's current state, it didn't. The digital experience it had going was firmly rooted in the internet's Brochure Age and its successor, the Digital Marketing Age. But a new plate shift had taken place. A third age was upon the company. That meant the depth and quality of the experience the parks were delivering every day were not meeting the expectations of an evolving customer base. It was becoming impossible to disentangle the park experience from the digital experience. Cedar Fair risked going the way of the T. rex.

We at Bloomreach came on board to help Cedar Fair make this transition. We helped it create a responsive, dynamic website that could collect data from myriad sources and deliver great experiences. We helped create intelligent mobile apps and ensured all digital touchpoints connected to personalized customer profiles. And with all that, plus a commitment to provide customers with the best vacation ever, Cedar Fair entered the new age of the internet, the Digital Business Age. At this point on the internet timeline, digital has evolved from a brochure to a marketing strategy to its latest form: a mandate that permeates every aspect of the business. Digital has burst its confines and has become part of everything a company does—no department is untouched. In this new age, the internet has shed its old image as a project of the technologists or a siloed marketing effort and has embedded itself into everything that is mission critical about a company. According to Jim, "People are passionate about these parks and they were happy to see that we were making an investment in them. It wasn't an investment in our technology; it wasn't an investment in all of the cool new tools; it was an investment in the guest experience."

The Cedar Fair evolution is a great example of what's happening in business now. Just as those of us in business shifted to embrace websites and online advertising, we now find ourselves in a new space—one in which digital is not a project but a mission that has taken over all aspects of the business. We are in the Digital Business Age, and it is overtaking everything business thought it had planned around the use of the internet. We have moved from brochure websites and digital ad campaigns to a new level of digital engagement. Now when you go to Cedar Point, the app is your companion. It tells you the wait time on your ride, it offers you a Fast Lane to the front of the line, it collects and distributes the benefits of your loyalty program, and it enables you to order food and plan your next activity. The digital experience and the park experience are one and the same. The wall between the digital and the real worlds has fallen. Digital is now everything you do.

The way this remakes the work of a company—any company—cannot be overstated. In the early days, a tech team cared about the

Web, so a website was under IT. In the advertising age, a marketing team cared a lot about digital, so the digital team was under marketing. In this third age, the digital team knows no departmental boundaries. Digital is permeating everything from payments to orders. Digital connects to loyalty programs and to suppliers. Employees are logging on to figure out when their shifts are scheduled. Digital is not a project or even a department—it's a hub. It's the mandate that runs through everything I do as a businessperson every day. There is no part of a company that is untouched.

In the Digital Business Age, digital is no longer a sideshow or a cloistered activity of marketing; it's the heart of my entire business. It's as if I leveled my building and have now laid down an entirely new foundation for the new structure. The walls of this new world go up with digital bricks at the base. No longer is digital a pure customer-facing, front-end activity for customer service and sales. Now, in this third age, I am reexamining everything I do using a digital lens. My org chart changes. My technology changes. My operating model changes. My business model changes. My capital financing changes. Everything I do is different.

Cedar Fair is totally focused on offering a great experience at the parks, and digital is at the heart of it. It has embraced the latest in technology not only to help guests navigate easily but also to assist the inner workings of the company through data capture. And it has rethought the way digital is perceived in the 150-year-old organization. What was originally a project and then a department is now the foundation of everything the company does. The results have been significant.

It took a lot of 2016 for Jim and his team to launch the first park on the new digital experience platform, but then the team got eleven park websites and seven mobile apps on its platform in the first four months of 2017. The experience is profoundly different. "We've gotten to the point where our mobile app can walk you through the park, showing you where to go and letting you know instantly, not five minutes later, if you're going in the wrong direction. We have wait times, we have show times, you can store your season pass on there. We can send you targeted offers, whether you're in the park, out of the park, in a different geo-fence outside the park or near a beacon inside of the park." Data from across a guest's interactions, over 60 percent mobile, flow into a digital experience platform that makes sense of the information and delivers a real-time personalized experience. The work is not done. "Look at it [digital] just as you would building a park," Jim says. "You can't just build a handful of coasters and walk away. You have to maintain it and continuously improve all the pieces your guests interact with."

This from a company born not in the innovation labs of Silicon Valley but in the family vacations of Ohioans.

Every summer family cars still roll to the park along that same route in Sandusky, but Cedar Fair has mapped a new road ahead for itself. It's a new age and it comes with a new instruction manual. We start charting that road where all journeys should start—with a new way to look at and talk about your customer. We start with the seeker.

PUT THE SEEKER AT THE CENTER

We go to the internet because we seek something: love . . . adventure . . . education . . . opportunity . . . the hot new gadget . . . the must-have holiday toy . . . an escape from our daily life.

But when we get there, we find the internet is a frustrating place—because when it comes to choices, the internet has outdone itself. Fueled by the ever-accelerating rate of new data and new content, everyone out there can offer you a product or service that you should try. We are awash in options and left to wonder whether we might find something better with just one more click. The hunt for one item turns into a quest for answers amid far too many possibilities. Choice becomes distracting rather than focusing. Which is the best item for us? And how can we know?

We go to the internet for solutions, and instead we get a digital to-do list that forces us to try to optimally select each item on the list. It becomes a routine exercise in frustration. As experts encourage us to spend less time in front of our screens, we are only spending more. We don't know who to blame for our predicament. We're wondering why the internet isn't making us happier.

This is the challenge presented to digital teams. And to get rid of what frustrates us and create the winning experiences we want, the teams need a new way of looking at the problem—one that puts the seeker in the center.

We can define *seeker* as a customer or consumer looking to achieve a higher-order outcome—which then gets decomposed into a series of products or services that they might be looking for. They then become a customer or prospect looking for those products and services.

All over the internet, you'll find businesses and organizations reorienting the user experience to put the seeker at the center. These companies recognize that while choice is great, we can do much more to make the experience positive and productive.

Some pioneers in the seeker-centric movement are deeply connected to the unhappiness that lies just beneath the surface of many internet interactions. Julie Bornstein is a former COO of Stitch Fix—a fashion retailer designed for people who think the internet has ruined shopping. "It's hard to shop. It's gotten to a point where

Figure 2.1 Stitch Fix serves the fashion seeker. Shutterstock.

shopping is overwhelming," she says. "Even if you're a really savvy shopper, it's exhausting and inefficient."

I've known Julie for many years, and in that time, she has made many stops on her career journey to fix apparel and fashion digital shopping—growing up at Nordstrom; then at Urban Outfitters, Sephora, and Stitch Fix; and now at her own fashion start-up, The Yes, which she cofounded with former Bloomreach chief technology officer Amit Aggarwal. She started in e-commerce in the days when the mission was simple: put a product catalog online and allow people to transact. Eventually that mission would get extended to add more and more products and make it easier and easier for customers to shop. But ten years after being an e-commerce pioneer, she got involved in Stitch Fix, where the approach was exactly opposite that of Nordstrom, Urban Outfitters, and Sephora. It was not about having more product online; it was about having less product, having a more personalized experience, and having the shopping done for you. Her newest venture, The Yes, goes one step further as it attempts to marry the benefits of a vast selection across brands with personal recommendations and a custom-ranked search for each shopper.

Julie is not alone. Rent the Runway, another fashion destination, was started with the fundamental insight that many women simply don't want to wear the same outfit often—an observation that has led to fast-fashion success stories like H&M and Zara. But Jennifer Hyman and Jennifer Fleiss started Rent the Runway on the premise that maybe outfits don't always need to be bought—maybe they can be rented. Many years after they founded their business, their customers wear rented outfits over 120 days a year! The first generation of fashion businesses on the internet—Nordstrom, Macy's, and others—focused on offering more and higher-quality choices. They were followed by the fast-fashion players such as Zara and H&M that offered luxury brands knocked off at lower prices. The innovators looked deeper and decided that the seeker's true motivation was wanting to look great, to vary their outfits, and to be true to their style and fit—all with minimum effort. They delivered that experience and built multibillion-dollar enterprises along the way.

Designing for the seeker isn't just about fun and fashion. Nowhere might the impact of a seeker-centric experience be more profound than in health care. I discovered the revolution in health care first-hand by speaking to Roger Donald, who has been a Bloomreach customer for many years and has spent the better part of ten years reinventing the digital offerings at one of the world's largest health care organizations—the UK's National Health Service (NHS) and its digital arms, NHS Direct (retired as an organization in 2014) and NHS Digital. He describes the problem NHS is trying to solve as "relevance and context"—more specifically, choosing which item from among four hundred digital product and service offerings to put in front of the user at a particular time. NHS serves a very wide range of personas—from physicians and nurses to government officials and research organizations. But no one is more central than the patient.

One of the first digital undertakings was the NHS Direct Health and Symptom Checkers, which allowed patients to triage their

Figure 2.2 NHS answers the question: What do I do next? Shutterstock.

symptoms so that they can be directed toward an appropriate level of care increasing choice and leading ultimately to better medical outcomes. But NHS did not stop there. They asked themselves the deeper question: "Why does someone go to the doctor in the first place?" Of course, the answer is because they feel ill. But how can they know if they should get a good night's sleep and they will feel better in the morning or if their symptoms warrant an immediate visit to the emergency room? The internet is littered with questionable medical advice. But NHS wanted to get to the heart of the issue. It wanted to harness the expertise and data it had across a wide range of symptoms and diagnoses to create a true self-serve symptom checker. And it wanted a checker that would directly meet the patient's goal: to understand their ailment and determine what to do next. "It might tell you to go down to the chemist and get some ibuprofen and you'll be fine in a couple of days. Or it might give you another outcome: we advise you to speak to your doctor in the next couple of days—or to call an ambulance because you need help right now," says Roger. The technology takes clinical algorithms and allows patients to interact with them to get guidance. It's a lot more efficient than googling your symptoms and hoping for a good answer.

The NHS technology doesn't treat you as a patient of any one kind of service; rather, it treats you as a seeker of advice on what to do next when faced with a health issue. The self-serve Symptom Checker doesn't just have to meet the bar of being right—it needs to provide accurate and comforting advice. The seeker is, more than anything, looking for reassurance that the path they go down is the best option available. Would customers have told NHS that it should apply AI and its database to build a symptom checker? Unlikely. When hospital patients are surveyed, they complain about a wide range of issues ranging from receiving unsatisfactory nursing care to feeling unengaged in their care. But nowhere do the surveys reveal that patients would prefer not to go to the hospital or doctor's office at all. That's because by the time those surveys would have been conducted, the seeker's original intentions would have been lost, and they would have already turned into a digital customer.

Seeker is more than just another word for *customer*. A seeker has a higher order of intention. Before you are a customer, you are a human being with a want or a need.

A seeker has a purpose they intend to fulfill, a task they want to complete. It can be mastering a skill, booking a memorable vacation with their family, feeling healthier, or buying a home. A seeker decomposes their intentions into a series of digital tasks and then becomes a potential customer of multiple products and services. Behind every customer is a seeker, calling out to you to satisfy their higher-order intention—to help them buy just the dress for an occasion or find a reassuring diagnosis in the middle of the night.

It's not a call everyone is ready to hear. More often than not these days your internet experience will be frustrating or disappointing. You may find what you want, but it's just as likely you will get tired of searching and settle for whatever looks best so far. You'll just cross your fingers, click, and hope for the best. This is because so much of the online experience today is designed to be customer centric—in other words, to sell you something in the most friction-free manner possible. It is a concept designed to separate you from your money with maximum efficiency, both for you and for the seller. Now sometimes you may want that level of efficiency. But not always. And plenty of times you want something far more personal than efficiency. Who serves you then? Much of the frustration we experience on the Web stems from a desire to offer choice. But choice means a transfer of work from the provider of the service to the consumer of the service. Search on Google and find millions of results to choose from. Check your news feed on Facebook and the scrolling continues indefinitely. Look for a gift on Amazon. Good luck. The idea was for the Web to be the place where anything can be found. And that's exactly the problem. In a place where everything is available, nothing can be found.

The change is taking place across industries. My friend Sam Shank asked, "Why do you need my product?" in the early days of starting HotelTonight, a travel business he eventually sold to Airbnb. He was a veteran of the travel industry, which was then littered with the Travelocities and the Expedias—places you could go to book a trip.

They did the two things that so many internet experiences had mastered. They figured out how to give you an unlimited number of places you could go (choice), and they enabled you to book that trip in a matter of minutes (efficiency). But Sam asked a different kind of question: "Why are people booking that vacation?" What he discovered was that there are many different kinds of trips people want to take, and the planned trip is only one kind. In fact, in the history of travel, a significant percentage of it is spontaneous, not planned. And the digital experiences offered by Expedia and Travelocity assumed you wanted to plan a trip, not get up and go. For him, the seeker was seeking a place to sleep right now. And in many ways, he sees his product not as a new element but as a throwback. "Planning is a construct of the last one hundred years—before trains, we didn't rely on clocks and calendars. If you think about it, spontaneous is the way we as human beings would prefer to operate," he says.

Sam's focus on the spontaneous traveler reveals a lot about the nature of the seeker. They will often have latent needs, rarely obvious from their interactions with the platforms they may currently frequent. They will settle for the digital products and services

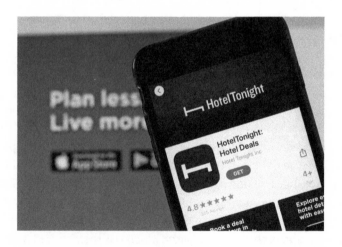

Figure 2.3 HotelTonight serves the spontaneous traveler. Shutterstock.

available, but ultimately they will become frustrated at the lack of congruence between their higher-order intention and the product or service on offer.

The notion of a higher order of intention isn't just a niche trend affecting a minority of the globe's digital consumers. It can profoundly change industries. We can see this taking place in real estate—an industry that impacts a wide swath of seekers. Seeker-centric entrepreneurs are reconfiguring the process, as we can see in Andreesen Horowitz general partner Alex Rampell's investment, Flyhomes.

Here's how Flyhomes works. Say someone puts their house up for sale, and ten people show up and want to buy it. One of those people has a lot of cash in their bank account; they can write a check right away. That person is going to get the house. One of the other nine may be willing to pay more, but they just don't have that cash in their bank account right now. They can apply for a mortgage, but what if the bank rejects them? The seller says, "I'm gonna go with the buyer who has all cash."

Flyhomes is a real estate brokerage—so it buys the house for you. This is a good idea that traditional realtors can't replicate. "It would be very hard for Joe the Real Estate Agent to do this unless Joe happened to have $5 million sitting around in his checking account. He can't say: 'I'll buy the house for you, you go get your mortgage, and you can pay me back in 45 days,'" says Alex.

I met Alex when he was an entrepreneur at Trialpay, an early financial technology start-up that he would later sell to Visa. Alex always saw digital opportunities through the lens of entire industries, not just single businesses. When he became a venture capitalist, he brought that thinking to the real estate industry. A few years later he is an investor across a set of start-ups trying to disrupt the real estate industry, including Point, Divvy, and Flyhomes. He believes that in the future, you won't be searching on Zillow and buying homes from brokers; you will be buying or selling homes, digitally, from a company, ultimately challenging the $100 billion in commissions made by real estate brokers across the United States. The pioneers in digital experiences for real estate, like Trulia and Zillow, can help you find your next property and assess what it might sell for. But that isn't what the seeker is seeking. The seeker is seeking to buy or sell a home. And these experiences fundamentally fall short. That's what has ushered in a new generation of seeker-centric disruptors, including Flyhomes (which buys the home for you), Opendoor (which buys your house from you), Divvy (which buys the house for you and then rents it to you), Point (which enables you to sell part of your house), and a very wide range of home-sharing companies that enable you to live with roommates in your house. All these businesses are powered by unique software and data-driven digital experiences that don't just help you with one part of the home-buying journey (searching for houses and understanding their prices); they go to the higher-order intention of the seeker—completing the transaction—and help the seeker get that job done. Indeed, in Alex's mind, this kind of full value-chain thinking will disrupt entire industries, not just create interesting companies.

Across all these industries, we are seeing the move from customer-centric to seeker-centric experiences. I saw the beginnings of this in the early days of founding Bloomreach. We started Bloomreach to enable the billions of people worldwide who were increasingly living their lives digitally to have the kind of magical experiences that get to the heart of what they are looking for. We fashioned our work as the flip side of the Google experience. When Google would give you seven million responses to a query, our question was, What's the point of returning a ton of blue links if when a user clicks through, they don't find exactly what they are seeking? Over twenty years after the founding of Google, search engines have trained us well. When we type in a query that doesn't get us what we are looking for, we assume that we typed in the wrong thing and start modifying our queries. Google is culprit #1 in inundating us with choice rather than giving us what we seek. Search companies see that clearly and are evolving search from results to answers, the boxes of information where they aim to give you what you are looking for without needing to click to a website.

I see Bloomreach brands that are winning reimagine their digital experiences away from just serving the customer better to meeting the seeker where they are. What they are trying to do is not incremental. They are rethinking with digital at the center by changing the fundamental questions of business. Instead of "What do you want?" they are asking "Why are you here?" They are shifting from a customer-centric thinking that pushed them primarily to improve the customer experience. Instead, they are digging for an underlying problem. At Bloomreach, we've extended our business to meet the demand for seeker-centric experiences. Search is still at the core of Bloomreach. But we have extended the capabilities of the platform to go beyond what we would have traditionally described as *search* to deeply understand who the user is and give them an experience that's uniquely suited for them.

A great example of that is a company Bloomreach works with called Uncommon Goods. Go to the Uncommon Goods website, and you won't see the usual e-commerce home page. Instead, you'll see a gift-finder chatbot that doesn't start with what you are shopping for but rather with the person you are shopping for. Uncommon Goods uses Bloomreach's relevance technology to power a gift-giving chatbot, understanding clearly that while the customer may be looking to buy a gift, the seeker is looking to delight a friend or loved one. It offers its products in a conversational interface, understanding that normal human behavior involves interaction, not just multiword queries.

While Uncommon Goods was busy reimagining gift giving, FC Bayern Munich, another Bloomreach customer, was reimagining the most popular sport in the world—soccer. Bayern started as a Bavarian football club, and in many ways, it still is. Except that while Bavaria has a total population of thirteen million people, FC Bayern has six hundred million global fans, making it one of the largest sports franchises in the world. I got to know the Bayern story by meeting Benjamin Stoll, who was head of digital strategy, platforms, and innovation at Bayern Munich. His story reminds us that fundamentally seekers are people, each unique and each with a highly personal connection to their favorite football club. Seekers want to participate in the experience, not just consume it. Soccer is a personal passion

Figure 2.4 For Bayern Munich, fan engagement is key. Shutterstock.

for hundreds of millions of people, most of whom will never make it to see a game at the beautiful Allianz Arena. So Benjamin and his team at Bayern created a new kind of experience—one that leveraged augmented reality to enable any fan to take an image of their favorite player and transpose it to interact with them in their location of choice. They could create a selfie with Manuel Neuer and Arjen Robben and configure and buy personalized jerseys. It is about emotional participation through the power of technology, Stoll says.

A winning digital experience starts with a seeker-centric offering. Winning digital teams embrace this orientation right away. When considering the offering, they don't ask "What?" They ask "Why?"

"What?" is the question that most businesses address. What does my customer want? It's the obvious starting point for a business or organization that offers a product or service.

To create a winning digital experience, we want to shift that thinking away from a product or service and instead create an offering that is an experience encompassing the product or service. To get to that experience offering, we have to move up the traditional sales funnel. We don't want to ask the customer what they want. We want to ask them why they've come to us. It's the "why" question that will tell us how to create the best offering.

Think of a fashion e-commerce site. The customer comes to your site and is navigating the site, perhaps using the search function, looking for a dress. In this scenario, it's reasonable to assume the "what" for this customer is a dress. But do we know the "why"? If we do, we can do a much better job for this individual.

Suppose we can ask why the customer has come to our site. Now we can learn the customer is shopping for an interview outfit ... or a cocktail dress for a business trip ... or a dress for a destination wedding. That helps us. But if we keep asking "Why?" we get even more.

Perhaps the customer is here because she's price sensitive and she's looking for a deal. Or she's pressed for time and she wants to get this done in a hurry. Or she doesn't really know what she wants, but she's hoping for fashion advice.

All these "why" questions get us so much more information than the "what" questions ever could.

It's important to note that seeker centricity isn't just about cool, fun, and helpful experiences. I see the seeker-centric phenomenon creating tremendous economic value all around us. We see that in juggernauts like Uber and Airbnb. Uber was not just another taxi service. It was the answer for the individual seeking transportation. Instead of the traveler going out and finding a taxi, Uber put the seeker at the center and in control of the experience. The car comes to you. Airbnb is not a booking engine or a hotel; it's a service that enables you to stay in unique places and do unique things. Operating at the higher order of intention has created tens of billions of dollars in market capitalization.

Becoming seeker centric is not a simple transformation. When you address a seeker, you may find that what they're seeking goes far beyond what you as a business offer. Businesses may find they must look beyond a traditional roster of products and services and ask "What could we possibly assemble, what could we possibly provide, that gets as close as possible to what the seeker is seeking so they have to do as little work as possible to achieve that goal?" It's no small consideration.

That said, the advent of seeker centricity has opened a huge opportunity—one that start-ups and legacy companies alike can exploit. When we talk about who's at the forefront now, it's the new companies that have no baggage and no legacy. But actually the companies with existing assets are in a stronger position to pull this off. You may have a bunch of companies in Silicon Valley building new insurance companies and new banks and even new grocery stores. But who better to pull off new banks, new insurance companies, and new grocery stores than existing ones? Existing companies already have the customer, the supply chain, and the brand credibility. In order to win, they need to stop asking "What?" and start asking "Why?" This opportunity is not just for the Silicon Valley start-ups. It's a chance for every business to reframe its outlook and serve the seeker.

How do we untangle the seeker concept from its predecessor, the customer? Excellent question—and that's our next topic.

3

SWAP CUSTOMERS FOR SEEKERS

What's the difference between customer-centric and seeker-centric thinking?

Understanding the difference between the two terms—and the two experiences they offer—is the best way to understand who is winning the digital arms race and who is about to be left behind.

Converging trends have forced this question of customer centricity versus seeker centricity. We live in a time of volatility and disruption, fueled by a rising flow of available capital. No business can assume its market is safe. A study by PWC found executives deeply worried about disruption—and not just from potential competitors. More than three-quarters of CEOs feared their customers would be their most disruptive force, pushing back on everything from pricing to corporate responsibility. If once upon a time convenience and brand loyalty kept shoppers happy, today their eyes are opened to what is new and engaging. Your best customer is only a click away from sampling your rival.

In this high-pressure environment, organizations are forced to face the evolution in internet possibilities. The job of creating a winning digital experience that attracts and keeps customers is harder than ever.

Table 3.1

Customer-Centric Versus Seeker-Centric Behaviors

	Customer-Centric	Seeker-Centric
Key question	*How* can we serve you better?	*Why* are you looking for our product or service?
Intention	Complete a task	Fulfill a goal
User feeling	Choice	Simplification
Offering	Product or service	Experience
Business model	Sale of product or service for a fixed price	Subscription or outcome driven
Technology	Suite of technology products	Open platform
Key roles	Functional (sales, marketing, IT, etc.)	Experiential + integrated (product management, design, engineering)
Key impact	Customer service, sales	"Whole offering"
Financial metric	EBITDA margin	Lifetime value of the customer
Emotion	Satisfaction	Exhilaration
User frame of mind	Slow thinking	Fast thinking
Competition	Others who offer your product or service	Substitute offerings that meet your customer's goal
Ultimate competitive advantage	Focused excellence	Ecosystem
Testing	Voice of the customer	Latent needs, testing, experimentation
Secret weapon	Capability	Culture

The move from customer-centric to seeker-centric thinking may sound like a slight change, but it's actually a paradigm shift. It's the difference between fixing a flat tire and inventing a hoverboard. When you break down the two concepts, the differences become more obvious—and inspiring.

ASK THE KEY QUESTION

Any internet engagement starts with someone approaching an organization's site or app or other digital experience.

A customer-centric experience asks: How can we serve you better?

A seeker-centric experience asks: Why are you looking for our product or service?

These key questions reveal an important split in philosophy. The customer-centric experience assumes that there is a concrete answer to its question. When customer-centric thinking came into vogue, the process of asking the customer what they wanted became the guiding principle. We as customers were constantly offered surveys, feedback opportunities, and options to rate and review. These are all tools of the customer-centric trade. They reveal quite of a bit of good information, but they are never going to make much headway in getting to the heart of a transformational digital experience.

The reason these tools fall short is no secret. We are just not that good at expressing what will make us happy. Henry Ford faced this when he rolled out the Model T. He famously dinged customer-centric thinking by observing that if he quizzed his customers on what they really wanted, they would have told him they wanted faster horses. Customers, Ford knew, do not always articulate the path to happiness. Their concrete answers gloss over the bigger issues plaguing their everyday lives.

For this reason, asking "How can we serve you better?" will unleash a flood of requests—discounts, faster checkout, secret sales—none of which profoundly improves the muddled, complicated, time-consuming internet experience. They are little prizes offered to the customer for hanging in there. But they are not a step up in digital experience.

On the other hand, a seeker-centric experience poses a different key question. By asking "Why?" it engages on a higher level. Let's think of it in terms of one of the companies we introduced in chapter 2—Stitch Fix. The customer-centric question a clothing site might ask is "How can we better help you buy a dress from us today?" Stitch Fix embraces the seeker-centric key question: "Why are you looking for a dress from us?"

And that "why" question can unleash a flood of information the customer-centric experience would never see: Your cousin's wedding is next month and you have nothing to wear. Worse, this is the judgmental side of your family and they'll be looking for gossip fodder. You're not looking forward to it. You need a new dress.

Customer centricity generates a coupon for a dress or a really large selection of dresses to choose from. Seeker centricity connects the shopper with a stylist for the dress.

Both result in a dress purchase. Which customer is happier and ultimately more loyal?

KNOW THE TRUE INTENTION

Seeker and customer have different intentions.

The customer is an individual on a mission. And we have all been that person. You're going to the grocery store to get milk. You're going online to order a specific book. You're buying a ticket—the date, time, and destination are already set. In customer mode, we are acting to complete a task. We know what that is, and what we want from any company or organization is ease of completion. Just as when you approach the checkout counter, your shopping cart full of food, you want the line to move quickly, so, too, do we hope our buying process will be smooth and simple. This is the customer nirvana.

That said, we are not always customers. Sometimes—indeed, oftentimes—we are seekers. In seeker mode, we have a different intention. We are not acting to complete a task. We are acting to fulfill a goal. It sounds similar, but in practice, it is a different universe of behavior. Customers have zeroed in on a product or service. They are ready to buy and leave. Perhaps the most recent of Amazon's many customer-centric innovations is Amazon Go, the supercool micro-grocery store that allows you to walk in, scan your Amazon app with its Prime subscription, pick up something off the shelf, and walk out. Walmart takes this further, delivering those groceries directly into my fridge. Maximum efficiency to purchase.

But before the grocery shopper became an Amazon customer, they were a seeker of a good meal for the family who went through the process of deconstructing that meal into a series of ingredients and putting them on a shopping list for a future grocery store visit. The seeker in us just wants to produce that great meal. Digital experience cooking services are trying to bring us that quality of experience. Blue Apron is concerned not with the narrow goal of making an individual sale but with the broader goal of providing what could be called a "whole offering." You're not just buying chicken; you're buying a dinner solution. Amazon may succeed at making grocery shopping more efficient, but if Blue Apron succeeds, we may not need to visit Amazon Go or sign up for Walmart's delivery of ingredients—at least not with the same frequency we once did.

UNDERSTAND USER EMOTION

How are you today? How are you really?

How you are feeling matters. At least it should. When you approach a brand's experience, the feeling you carry with you into the process should inform the experience.

When users approach in a customer-centric mode, what they want is choice. They've already decided to buy black boots. The question now is, Who will close that transaction? To answer that, the user must make a choice.

25

Choice has been a powerful driver for e-commerce—and one of the primary reasons for its popularity. While we were once limited to the choices and abilities of our local merchants, the internet gave use choice as we'd never imagined it. We could choose not just from among the black boots stocked at my local shoe store but also from among all the black boots stocked anywhere in the world. All of it was now available to us, and the options were thrilling.

But while the thrill of the hunt can be fun for some, it's a burden to most.

When it comes to emotional priority, seekers don't demand choice. What they'd like is a highly curated, personalized experience. The seeker values simplicity. So, yes, I'd love to be able to choose from a wide selection of black boots—but every option in the world? Maybe that's more than I need to be made happy. What if the merchant could understand my preferences—and my user feeling of simplicity—and provide me with a selection that meets my needs instead of dumping a hundred pages of SKUs into my search results?

We can see the power of this profoundly through the Symptom Checker that Roger Donald and his team at NHS Direct built.

Imagine you're a patient in England and the NHS has two options: it can give you an extensive amount of literature on symptoms, likely ailments, and likely remedies, or it can give you the Symptom Checker app, perhaps ultimately tied to your electronic health record. Scouring through scary health risks is emotionally painful. Quickly getting to some level of accurate understanding of whether you need to be heading to the ER or sleeping off an ailment brings you the comforting feeling of at least knowing where you stand. Indeed, experiences that cater to the seeker's desire for simplicity bring joy, reassurance, and closure.

Perhaps one of the biggest and most important splits between customer centricity and seeker centricity comes in the concept of emotional outcome. What is a customer-centric company looking for in an emotional outcome? It's not a deeply hidden answer: customer satisfaction. Indeed, satisfaction has been the emotional goal for business for generations. Satisfaction crept into advertising campaigns and training manuals: "Satisfaction guaranteed or your money back." "Always keep the customer satisfied." That was the aim: satisfaction.

Seeker-centric businesses take the position that *satisfaction* is a pretty low bar. Sure, you can be satisfied. But what if I told you that you could trade *satisfied* for *exhilarated*? This is the promise of seeker centricity.

To understand the differing frame of mind in play here, we can look at the work of economist and author Daniel Kahneman. In his book *Thinking, Fast and Slow*, he generates the central thesis that there are two key modes of thought: System 1 is fast, instinctive, and emotional; this is what we term *fast thinking*. System 2 is slower, more deliberative, and more logical; this is *slow thinking*.

In traditional retail, the power of fast thinking is on display all the time. Think about a time when you stopped at the supermarket for something you purchase routinely—cereal, bread, soda. You likely entered the store, made straight for the appropriate aisle, and snatched your item off the shelf. Did you make the best choice? Maybe, maybe not. But you didn't engage in a long, thoughtful decision-making process about which brand of bread would you make you happy. You grabbed the brand you like. And the brand is what creates the fast-thinking experience. There are a dozen brands on the bread shelf, but the brand name (fueled by its advertising campaign) did the sorting for you and gave you a shortcut.

Who does the sorting for you online? A seeker-centric operation looks to adopt fast thinking by understanding your mission and creating shortcuts for you. The seeker business bets you will like that better than sorting through pages of Google results.

When it comes to understanding the difference between customer centricity and seeker centricity, the fast and slow systems of thinking provide a robust illustration. Customer-centric companies lean on slow thinking—the process is deliberative, follows a set path, and takes a good bit of our time to navigate. By contrast, a seeker-centric experience is more tuned to fast thinking. The experience created by the seeker-centric business endeavors to be fast and instinctive and to require less effort, organization, and research on the user's part.

TURN YOUR OFFERING INTO
A DATA-INSPIRED EXPERIENCE

One of the most important differences between customer-centric and seeker-centric businesses comes in the offering itself.

For generations, the offering of any business was a product or service. This represented the full selection of options. When you came to market, you offered your product or service for sale, and customers decided if they wanted to buy.

The advent of seeker-centric thinking brings a third option to the marketplace. That is the experience, these days delivered digitally. Indeed, I started Bloomreach because I fundamentally believe that digital experiences are at the heart of where we all live as human beings. More and more of our customers have stopped thinking about their individual websites or mobile apps and have started to think of the experience as the fabric of interaction that they offer.

Joseph Pine, in his work defining and demystifying the experience economy, demonstrated that business could make a leap when it could understand that not everyone who walks through the doors simply wants a product or service. The founders of the American Girl stores realized the merchandise was only half the story. Girls and their families came for the experience—complete with a beauty salon, restaurant, and live entertainment. Apple stores were designed to invoke the vibe of a boutique hotel. Digital interaction needs to make that leap. Most things the seeker is looking for require an experience. That experience doesn't have to be a synonym for entertainment. This is not about how much fun you can have online. The seeker-centric experience may or may not be entertaining.

Let's think about experience in a way that is less theatrical. You've recently had knee surgery and you're laid up, recovering. But you're out of milk. Then you remember your local grocery store has recently introduced drone delivery. Two clicks and twenty minutes later, milk is at your doorstep. In this scenario, your grocer has offered you a seeker-centric solution. Yes, you are a customer for milk. But before that, you were an individual with a bad knee and two cranky kids wanting milk for their cereal. Your higher purpose is to overcome your knee issue and still take care of your family. The drone provides that experience for you—the act of sitting home and awaiting your airborne delivery. It's the experience that makes the sale.

We have long been trained to expect either a product or a service as an offering. We are only just learning that this third option—experience—is even available to us. Experience is a key way a company can disrupt a marketplace—providing an offering we never imagined.

If you want to create this higher level of offering, how do you go about it? The answer is in data—all of it.

We live in a time when data surrounds us. Everything we do—our search habits, our shopping habits, our travel habits, our communications habits—throws off data. If I take a break from writing today and go get a flat white at Starbucks, I've generated all manner of data. The Starbucks location will harvest my purchase data, my purchase history, and whether or not I was persuaded by a new product advertised in-store. The security cameras in the parking lot will capture my face and how I traveled to the location. A mapping app will record my route. My smart watch will generate the level of activity I exhibited. My computer will note the length of time I spent away from my work. My social media may record my mood at the moment of purchase. And if, instead of making a physical trip, I opted to take my work break by shopping for something online, the data potential explodes. My clicks will tell you how I browsed, if I purchased, what I rejected, what never got me to click at all, my click and purchase history, and my demographic profile. This is true even if I never made a purchase at all.

All our actions generate data that leave our devices and circulates in the virtual atmosphere. This is true whether or not you participate in social media or click "No" on boxes that purport to guard your privacy. In the era we inhabit, our data billows off us like steam. While that may seem alarming, it can work to our benefit as seekers. And if you are in the business of creating a seeker-centric offering, your road map is in the data.

Data can be gleaned in what I'll call the traditional manner. You can set up focus groups and conduct interviews. This is the data collection process that has been used for generations. You may pick up some important insights in this process. Your focus group may yield usable data. Someone in the group may even have the self-awareness to express higher-level seeker thinking that will guide you forward. But relying on a select group of individuals to understand their needs and wants well enough to deliver what you need to create an offering is a difficult and time-consuming task. The better and more available answers exist in clicks—in the machine data—not behind one-way mirrors.

You don't need to conduct individual interviews; you need to look for patterns in the data. They are in every click, every search, every minute spent in front of a screen. In the data lie the signals consumers are offering that enable you to identify who they really are and what they are seeking. Every click on a website is a vote; every nonclick is a nonvote. This is the data that makes up your offering blueprint.

We engage in this process at Bloomreach all the time. If I show people eight links and most of them click only on link three, my next steps are written in data: I should move the one that's in the third position up to the top of the screen and the second one down. That's listening to a click, but the information provided hardly stops at the single click. In an individual visit, I can see all the things you purchase, all the things you don't purchase, your demographic data, and your past purchases. That's the data I can harvest by interacting with you online.

That's just the start. Data about who you are and what you want extends far beyond interaction. Consider the act of substitution. What if the data I am looking at says you didn't buy my product, and you didn't even make a purchase in my industry—but you substituted an entirely different purchase to solve your personal problem?

Suppose I'm a car manufacturer, and instead of buying one of my cars, you opted to put your money into a substitution option—Uber or Lyft. That tells me something about who you are, what you want, and why you considered—but ultimately rejected—my offering. You want a car because you want to get from point A to point B. Offerings that focus on the pleasure of driving or the value of gas mileage fall flat for you. You want a ride. But what you *seek* is an efficient, on-demand ride. That led you to a ride-sharing service and away from my offering of a fuel-efficient or high-performance car. Your actions give me the data I need to see not just what you did but also why you did it. Now I can envision a segment of consumers who may consider me—if I have the right offering. The data tells me my competition is not the auto dealership next door and whatever discount it may be offering during its Presidents' Day sale—it's the app in the palm of the traveler's hand. A focus group where I ask what kind of features drivers want in an automobile will give me some insights, but their clicks on the Uber app will be far more instructive.

Job one is making sense of the data.

That's not always easy. Too often businesses will home in on the good news data and fail to embrace the bad news data as instructive. Everyone loves to interview their fans. To use an example of a typical e-commerce site, say 5 percent of people who come to the site add something to a cart, and 1 percent buy something. That's another way of saying that one in one hundred people buy something. So now you look at the people who buy, and you ask "What can I learn from that?"

That's good data, to be sure, but it's likely to miss the seeker question. The one in one hundred who purchased from you liked everything about your offer enough to purchase. The ninety-nine, on the other hand, had enough incentive to visit but not enough to make a purchase. It's the ninety-nine who can tell you what you need to know to create a seeker offering. The ninety-nine can answer the higher-level question of "Why?" They can tell you that earlier in their consideration process, before they made their decision not to buy your widget, they were seeking something. They know what your offering should be. To create your offering, you need to step back: you go from the one who purchased, back to the five who abandoned their full cart, and then back to visitors who never clicked to add a product to their cart—the ones who searched and browsed but never got to your widget.

Why? What were they seeking?

Gathering this data allows you to create a bull's-eye view of your customer base. As you listen to the data and try to make sense of the higher-order "why" questions, you are developing a list of attributes of your customer base. The customers who love you and make purchases show you all the attributes of your fan base. They're your core. Then you start eliminating attributes to create the concentric target circles. With each step out of the bull's-eye, you are seeing fewer of the core attributes. Yet they all share the "why" that should shape your offering.

As you come out of the data harvest and begin to create your offering, consider this quick warning about using the popular Lean Startup concept of the MVP—the minimum viable product. The MVP is a staple of the start-up world—and for good reason. It's the bedrock of the try–fail–try again process, and it's the reason great ideas get out into the public sphere for comment and testing rather than languishing behind the walls of R&D for months, if not years. The MVP is a powerful concept with a notable track record. That said, it could threaten the search for the seeker offering.

When you're in the hunt for a seeker-centric offering, there is a danger in jumping too quickly to the MVP without fully considering the wider range of options. That's because once you pick an MVP, all your feedback will center on that initial offering. If you missed the right offering, you may never hear about it. Think of it this way: If you produce a play about World War II and start reading your reviews, the feedback may be positive or negative, but it's always going to be about the play you produced—the one about World War II. If the better offering was a play about space aliens, you're not going to get that news. You've narrowed your focus too early and cut yourself off from that information. You're on the wrong playing field. So, of course, you want an MVP, but don't rush there. Consider the variety of playing fields you can enter before committing to one.

When refining your offer, think hard about your bull's-eye customer. That's not your only customer, but it's the one for whom you want to optimize your offering. In the bull's-eye, seven out of ten visitors are buying your product or service. They love you. And this is critically important when it comes to evaluating the strength of your market share.

If I think I have a 20 percent market share in my category, that's huge. If I think I've got 50 percent, I'm practically a monopolist. That is how marketers tend to look at the landscape. They look at your market as a whole and all the possible people who could be interested in your offering. But they don't focus on the bull's-eye—and that's where your ultimate success lies. That's your highly loyal segment. There's nothing wrong with having some customers who come and go from your concentric circles. But your task is to optimize for the bull's-eye community. At the end of the day, to build a seeker-centered business, your seekers have to absolutely love you.

WHAT'S YOUR EDGE?

In the customer-centric world, it's easy to spot your competition. If you're a bank, your competition is other banks. If you're a restaurant, your competition is other restaurants. For generations, a business could often spot the competition coming and adjust to meet the new rival.

The seeker-centric world turns that truism on its head. Now others who offer your product or service are not your competition; instead, your competition resides in the mind of your customer. If you're a bank, your biggest threat is not another bank but the possibility that your customers will seek an alternative way to save or manage their money. If you're a restaurant, your competition is your customer seeking a new way to feed the family. As new seeker-centric businesses join the marketplace, customer-centric companies are finding it harder to keep an eye on the competition. Substitution looms as a much bigger risk than direct competition.

When a website or app serves only the customer, then the seeker is left to fend for themselves, and it's only a matter of time before someone serves them better. Like all disruptions, seeker-centric experiences start incrementally, often sneaking up on businesses. At first, the taxi industry looked at Uber as a black car service—only for the luxury traveler. For Priceline and Expedia, HotelTonight perhaps felt like a niche service—since spontaneous travel was likely a minority case for whimsical entertainment. But ultimately niche services that serve the seeker can start to be clear substitutes. The business traveler starts using the HotelTonight app or the average consumer starts developing the Uber habit, and then all bets are off.

Seeker-centric and customer-centric companies embrace different visions of the ultimate edge. For the customer-centric business, the edge is focused on excellence of delivery of a narrow product or service. The assumption is that if your product or service is better than everyone else's at meeting customer needs, you win. We know many companies that deliver excellent products and stand for quality: BMW in automobiles and Bose in speakers.

Seeker-centric businesses build an edge through the combination of many of the factors described above. Tesla embraced an alternate vision as its edge. Its initial cars may not have been engineered with the same quality as gas-powered cars, when measured by the traditional dimensions of automobile technology, but Tesla never defined itself as just another car company. It certainly built a great car, but its edge comes from being a great electric vehicle and from creating the emotional brand appeal that comes from feeling like you're part of the solution rather than the problem. Indeed, we are far from a place where that energy efficiency saves the consumer money when weighed against the price of the car. But Tesla was never competing on providing slow-thinking value to the customer—it was competing on meeting the seeker's desire to stand against the fossil fuel industry. The emotional resonance of the offering was strong—and it did not stop there. Step into a Tesla vehicle, and you will feel like you're interacting with an iPad, not a traditional automobile dashboard. Driving a Tesla is an experience—it provides the immediate fast-thinking impulse that comes with being transported to the future. To pull that off, Tesla had to view itself as a software company, a car company, an energy company, and a brand. It needed to integrate with several online services to enable you to issue a voice command that identifies the nearest coffee shop or requests a replacement part. Tesla's edge comes from a deep understanding of the seeker, a willingness to invest to make them a lifetime customer, the emotional resonance of its offering, and a willingness to think of its offering as much more than a car—as a driving experience.

AND THEREFORE . . .

So now we get to the important question: Who cares?

The answer to that is simple: any organization that uses technology to connect with its users.

The rise of seeker-centric thinking is remaking the reality in which you operate. It is opening your customers' eyes to an improved experience. It is giving your rivals a new edge in the business. It is creating a blank canvas for new competition to emerge. If competition used to be a straight-up arms race—whoever embraced the best new technology won the day—now the emphasis is not on invention but on a new way of creating experiences. Becoming seeker centric is the path to winning.

The new companies and services rising up around seeker centricity are not iterations of what we've known before—they are not just faster horses. Instead, they acknowledge that on our happiness scale, there is a notch above "satisfied" that customers are starting to discover. Those customers will reward the businesses that deliver this new level of happiness—in some industries, they are already doing so. Those businesses are the next generation of winners. Common to all of them is their ability to harness the modern digital experience technology stack.

4

HARNESS THE THREE AS

We've long used a game board to measure how close a computer could come to the workings of a human brain. We choose games, such as chess and Go, that we value as markers of our human intelligence, and then we take on artificial intelligence (AI) to see who is the master of the mind game. This is a long-running contest.

One of the key moments in this quest was the second challenge match in 1997 between Garry Kasparov, world champion and the strongest ever chess player until that time, and IBM's Deep Blue, in a high-stakes rematch. Kasparov had defeated Deep Blue previously and was very vocal and confident that computers would never match humans in playing chess. In a closely contested, highly controversial match, Deep Blue defeated Garry, and it started becoming clear that computers were going to be a force. At this point, however, Deep Blue was trained not only by software engineers but by professional chess players and it had studied every single game of Garry Kasparov. While it was a remarkable moment, the amount of human intelligence that was force-fed into Deep Blue was staggering. Chess was one thing, but Go was another. Defeating even strong amateurs in Go still seemed distant at best.

It took nearly two decades of AI development to build a Go engine that could defeat Lee Sedol, one of the world's strongest Go players.

The biggest difference between Chess and Go is simply that the space of possible moves in Go is so much larger than in Chess that you need to develop "intuition" into the software to be able to effectively enumerate the possible next moves. Passing this intuition from humans to engines without needing to explicitly write it in software was AlphaGo's main accomplishment. AlphaGo was developed by DeepMind, a UK company that had been acquired by Google. The second major AI advancement was that the main team that built AlphaGo, unlike Deep Blue, did not have very strong players to force-feed human knowledge. However, it was still trained with every single Go game played, and as a result every Go game that Lee Sedol had played. While this was an incredible accomplishment, what came next in 2018 dwarfs everything else.

In 2018, AI took a decidedly new turn. In December, the journal *Science* published a paper by DeepMind that catapulted the AI discussion into unexplored territory: Instead of being given access to reams of historical data on the games, AlphaZero, the new version of AlphaGo was simply given the rules of the game. That's it.

This was new. AI could teach itself—and quickly. Srinath Sridhar—a member of the founding engineering team at Bloomreach, an early engineer at Facebook, and later a founder of his own supply-chain optimization company, Onera—had spent his career in AI, starting with his PhD at Carnegie Mellon. Until that point, AI was based on historical data. The difference between AlphaZero and its predecessors was that it can learn from rules, just rules, he said. Suddenly AlphaZero could beat every human on the planet—learning that took humans thousands of years to amass and pass down from one Go master to their disciples all became stale in four hours thanks to AlphaZero. "It was mind blowing."

What does that moment in AI history say to us? It marks a point on the human timeline when machines could learn at a higher level—one that would allow them to recognize, communicate, and eventually create.

This matters for our discussion because AI is a critical—although not a singular—reason that winning experiences win. AI allows us to envision and execute deep seeker-centric experiences on the internet. But AI does not act alone. We need help to translate the breakthroughs attained in the research labs of DeepMind and the like into a consumer marketplace. We need more than a software chess master. We need a framework that allows the mind-blowing advances of AI to move into the world around us and function for our benefit. It's this collection of technological activity that we'll focus on in this chapter. This is the story of how technology trends converged to allow the winners to win big in digital.

We can understand the moment we are in with what I call the three As: AI, ambient technology, and application programming interfaces (APIs). Each of them is critical in its own right, but none of them alone created the opportunity we face today. It is the perfect storm of these technologies that both creates and propels the winning experience.

Each one brings its own magic to the tale.

Before this triple convergence, the story of the creation of your average digital experience on the Web is a pretty standard one. You do a bit of customer or user research—perhaps by interviewing some customers or conducting surveys. You then manually construct a website. You manually write the content—usually text, images, and videos. You manually upload that content into some kind of content management system or e-commerce platform. You hit "Publish" and admire the fact that you now have your unique place on the World Wide Web. But your chief financial officer asks you why your website isn't making money yet. So you start running some digital marketing programs—perhaps advertising on Google or Facebook. You get a newly minted MBA student to dig through Excel files of data—sales data, web analytics data, transaction data—to try to understand what is or isn't working. The data is rarely conclusive, so you might run some A/B tests on a couple of hypotheses. You continue to optimize that experience, hoping to serve your customers a little better and get a little bit closer to your business goals. The bigger your digital budget, the higher the level of sophistication, but ultimately the process of building, optimizing, and personalizing the experience has been pretty standard.

Table 4.1
The Three As

Artificial intelligence	The theory and development of computer systems able to perform tasks that normally require human intelligence, such as visual perception, speech recognition, decision-making, and translation between languages.
Ambient technology	A new world where computing devices are spread everywhere, allowing the human being to interact in physical world environments in an intelligent and unobtrusive way. These environments should be aware of the needs of people, customizing requirements and forecasting behaviors.
Application programming interface	A computing interface that defines interactions between multiple software intermediaries. It defines the kinds of calls or requests that can be made, the ways that these calls should be made, the data formats that should be used, the conventions that should be followed, etc.

But the three As have changed everything. We can imagine that the interplay among our three As bestows superhuman powers on us. Ambient interfaces represent our sensory organs—and we have just gotten superhuman sight, hearing, touch, and smell. AI is like a supercharged brain, making sense of it all at a scale and a speed never seen before. APIs in the cloud enable us to network that brain between each of us and with billions of other humans, ensuring that we can harness the crunching power and creativity of everyone else without needing to deeply understand how they each think and act. With these three, we evolve from testing and hoping to uncovering true intent and using that true intent to build winning experiences that serve the seeker.

ARTIFICIAL INTELLIGENCE

We start with AI since it's at the core of the change we're experiencing. AI has been with us for decades. It moved from our imaginations (think Frankenstein) to reality in 1940s with the theory of computation, which suggested that a machine could simulate any conceivable act of mathematical deduction. Researchers wondered whether a machine could show intelligent behavior, and the field of AI research was born.

But AI has come into its own as a practical means of identifying patterns and actualizing solutions in the last ten years with the combination of improved algorithms and systems that could affordably make this possible. Broadly speaking, AI is part of a larger continuum in the category of data science that stretches from statistical approaches to pattern matching to ML to supervised learning to unsupervised learning and general AI.

Samit Paul, Bloomreach's head of data science, has been a pioneer in the field for many years. He was working on data science and AI problems at GE Labs for the first decade of the 2000s—analyzing problems ranging from predicting wind turbine speed to analyzing mammograms. He ultimately made his way through both large organizations like American Express and Intuit and smaller software businesses like Yodlee and Bloomreach.

Samit argues that the fundamental nature of data science problems has not changed. They still involve exploring large data sets and building models to understand and optimize outcomes. But the limitations of cloud infrastructure, processing, and storage meant that the scale at which the models could operate has been dwarfed by the gargantuan clouds made famous by Microsoft Azure, Google Cloud Platform (GCP), and Amazon Web Services (AWS). At GE, Samit experienced the classic problem of text classification from field service reports on a range of GE's powered turbines. Technicians collected details on the state of the turbines, capturing them in field service reports, but how would one know which turbines needed parts replaced and which ones could wait? A human diagnosis may come too late. Samit and his team aimed to categorize those turbines through text classification, a technique in which field service reports are matched to a knowledge base of past malfunctions in order to automatically detect system vulnerabilities. But while the algorithms may have been sufficient, the available computing resources simply weren't. So Samit's team did what any practical group of researchers would do: they sampled. Rather than all the field reports, they used a representative sample of the data. Sampling is well understood, but its usefulness depends on how representative the sample is of the whole. The analysis could take days or weeks, and the conclusions could take months before they were put into effect. Today's AI-enabled clouds would crunch through those reports in near real-time and accurately direct the maintenance almost immediately.

As cloud infrastructure has evolved, putting the computing power of the giant internet companies in our hands, it has promoted the democratization of AI.

GCP consists of three pieces: an AI hub, described as a "hosted repository of plug-and-play AI components"; AI building blocks, which make it easy for "developers to add sight, language, conversation, and structured data into their applications"; and an AI platform, which lets "ML [machine learning] developers and data scientists take projects from ideation to deployment."

Indeed, AI is no longer the province of the rich and famous in the internet world. The best AI applications and platforms are now available to your average developer. In Google's and Amazon's clouds, the goal is to both enable the deployment of custom models and use prebuilt ones. All this democratization ultimately means velocity for a developer and a business. No longer should it take weeks or months to analyze wind turbine data. Using AI-powered text classification systems, experience builders can now iterate toward what the seeker is seeking at hyperspeed.

But AI hasn't just become more democratized—it has become a lot better.

AI was deployed as a visual assist when Google trained AI to identify cats in YouTube videos—evidence that software can learn, as the human brain does, to recognize and identify. What started with vision is equally applicable to text and voice. AI has brought us devices such as Amazon Echo and Apple Siri, which use speech recognition AI to respond to our voiced queries.

More recently, the pace of acceleration has only gotten more interesting as we move from classic ML models to a category of AI described as *deep learning*. In more classic ML approaches, data scientists will look for features in large data sets. In a problem involving sales forecasting or image identification, we set a goal (like maximize sales or identify the cat), and we then specify, often manually, the features that are most likely to matter in driving the goal. A feature of the image identification model may be its color. A feature of the sales forecasting model might be the past history of the sales rep. A data scientist will then select the right model, deploy it, and tune it—identifying the best fit. The ML model will crunch large amounts of data, often historical, picking the right features and their weights to optimize toward the desired outcome. These models work best when there are large data sets available. The assumption is that the past is an accurate predictor of the future.

But what happens when the features are really difficult to pick out? What happens when the past is not a great predictor of the future? This is where deep learning comes into play. Remember AlphaZero? Its ML predecessors would have mapped out every chess move, every countermove, and every past scenario to learn the right move. But AlphaZero could win the game just by understanding the rules, without all that historical data. It could do this because its deep learning system is able to learn all the dimensions that might influence an outcome, in effect learning the features without hypotheses and hints. It might identify a whole host of nonintuitive signals. Deep learning has the promise of breaking the tension in the classic ML paradox. You could typically take a very specific model—say one specifically built for sales forecasting—but it would fit only a very narrow problem case. Alternatively, you could take a more general model, but it would be hard to fit to the specific problem case. Because its techniques can deal with amorphous problem spaces, deep learning has the potential to solve many more problems—and in more precise, more accurate ways.

Why does all this matter to building seeker-centric digital experiences? To understand that better, we go back to the origin stories of Google and Facebook. Google started as a search engine—diligently working to "organize the world's information." Google has always stood for relevance. When you type your unstructured query into its search box, accompanied by its famous doodle, it seeks to scour the Web to return the most relevant ten blue links it can find for you. Facebook, on the other hand, is about giving "people the power to build community and bring the world closer together." While Google is about information, Facebook is about people. Facebook's origin story starts with the news feed—an assembly of highly personalized updates from friends and the rest of the Web. And herein lie the twin pillars of great digital experiences—relevance and personalization. It turns out that to deliver great relevance, who you are matters, but your intent, expressed as a query, matters even more. Google's ML and AI technology has been optimized for exactly that: deeply understanding every word you type in, how what you type matches a wide variety of documents, and what past users might have clicked on when they typed similar phrases into the search box. Facebook, on the other hand, applied its AI techniques to understand who you are, who you are connected to, and what you like. Today both Google and Facebook excel at personalization and relevance. Building great digital experiences requires one to conquer both. When the soccer fan that Bayern Munich was looking to serve interacts with the soccer team, the fan's favorite player and the activities of the fan's friends tell us a lot. On the other hand, if he is searching for a jersey, not distracting him with news of his favorite players would be a wise way to facilitate a transaction and get to the heart of what he seeks in that moment.

The Bloomreach story has been all about bringing the benefit of AI-powered relevance and personalization to every digital experience out there. We have always thought about digital experiences as a grand matching problem between demand and supply. The demand is expressed by the user—the soccer fan, the fashion shopper, or the sick patient. The supply is the assortment of products, services, and content that the brand has on offer—the custom jersey, the cat video, or the maintenance service. The job of our AI-powered engine is to ensure the right supply is presented to the right user at the right time on the right medium. Doing that requires a deep understanding of the user, their expressed intent (for example, what they type into a search box on a site we power), their implicit intent (maybe what they clicked on where they might be at a given moment), and a deep understanding of the catalog of supply. But the nuances of serving an individual brand make it quite different than serving a general population on the internet. While Google is aggregating across billions of internet users and Facebook has a deep profile of one individual, Bloomreach must build an AI system that can optimize the digital experiences of any business—including banks, soccer teams, fashion retailers, and government-powered health care. Doing that requires an expert system that is specific to the domain. Over the course of ten years of powering commerce on the Web, we have learned millions of synonym pairs—understanding that users seeking a *baby stroller* and an *infant stroller* are looking for the same thing, but that users seeking a *dress shirt* and a *shirt dress* are looking for wildly different products. We have learned what pieces of content lead to sign-ups, what products are bought together, and, while honoring data privacy, what level of price or brand affinity a given customer exhibits on one of the experiences we power. Indeed, while Google knows a little about everything and Facebook knows everything about you, Bloomreach knows exactly what you are seeking in the context of the brand you are interacting with.

But it isn't good enough to build relevant and personalized experiences. The goal of most digital experiences is to get users or customers to do something—to buy, sign up, read, watch, or take some other action digitally. AI comes to the rescue here as well. At Bloomreach, we build AI that, in addition to providing relevance and personalization, algorithmically optimizes for business outcomes. The Bloomreach AI will understand what products you have the highest probability of clicking on and buying, given who you are and how you have interacted with that brand. In addition, it will look across all customers and dynamically select the assortment of products, services, and content that maximizes revenue, margin, or other business outcomes. In doing that, we complete the story—we do what is right for both the seeker and the business.

Bloomreach is not alone in bringing AI to business optimization. Srinath's supply-chain optimization business, Onera, envisioned a refactoring of the retail supply chain. Historically, retailers had a simple set of rules to determine where to ship a product from once you ordered it. They typically tried to minimize the number of packages they sent to you and aimed to ship from the closest location. But ultimately those simple rules are really proxies for what the business is seeking to accomplish. The underlying motivation of the retailer is to minimize its cost and maximize the customer's happiness. So Srinath's team set out to optimize against those underlying goals by factoring in a much wider set of inputs—the loyalty of the customer, the likelihood of the product being marked down or replenished, and even the predicted lifetime value of the customer. AI can account for a much wider range of factors than any human being could.

The kind of AI-powered applications that Facebook, Google, Amazon, Bloomreach, and Onera build are available to every digital experience builder out there. On top of that, the democratization of even the most advanced AI techniques means that any organization or business can build AI-powered digital experiences—and should.

I witnessed that democratization firsthand through my interactions with the United States Tennis Association (USTA), where I serve as a member of the Champions Council for their player development arm. I played competitively in my younger days and have remained connected to the sport ever since. The USTA is the preeminent organization that promotes American tennis; in addition to running the U.S. Open, it has a goal to promote U.S. tennis champions. I got involved in the USTA through my interactions with Martin

Blackman, who leads the player development team there. Martin is a former U.S. tennis pro, ranked as high as 158 in the world. The USTA player development function he inherited lagged those of the other Grand Slam nations—Australia, the UK, and France—in its use of AI and analytics to drive athlete performance. He recounts what it was like from the time when he was playing until about ten years ago. A coach would video his matches or practices and then break down the film with him—perhaps watching all or parts of the video and identifying interesting moments. The coach would use their best judgment to break down the athlete's technique, relying on years of training and expertise. But Martin believed there should be a different way. He recruited Dave Ramos to build a performance analytics team, and in partnership with IBM Watson, they set out to revolutionize tennis in the United States.

The first problem to solve was how to identify interesting moments in a tennis match. Watching video of match after match was inefficient and time consuming. Using data from the Hawk-Eye system that captures video at major tennis events, the first generation of IBM's Watson system would identify interesting moments acoustically: more crowd noise might evidence interesting opportunities to "tag the data." Gradually, though, the AI system would get more and more sophisticated, auto-tagging everything from shot placement to swing trajectory and ball speed. The use of AI has enabled Martin, Dave, and the USTA team to transform how they deliver analytics to athletes. Martin breaks down the effects in three dimensions—technical, tactical, and developmental. On a technical level, the USTA team was able to put its coaching philosophy into software. Coaches could document the perfect forehand, and the AI system could detect deviations from that perfect form for any athlete. No longer was improvement gated by watching video serially and acting on a coach's judgment; the USTA system could process the sixteen thousand athletes who had come through its facilities, providing immediate technical feedback. Second, the system could provide tactical advice. Dave tells the story of the 2017 Women's Federation Cup match where one of the U.S. athletes was playing an unscouted

Czech opponent. The system determined that the opponent would never hit a serve to one particular corner of the service box, and this tactical advice enabled the U.S. player to anticipate every serve!

Finally, the promise of AI will enable the player development team to extend into developmental domains—identifying opportunities to improve mental or physical development, practice schedules, or nutrition opportunities. Fundamentally, sports and data science have found a symbiosis in incredible results. In a world where 1 percent better could be the difference between being outside the top one hundred in the world and being within the top ten, AI has made an impact.

The USTA story challenges misconceptions about AI. Much of the discussion around AI has centered on the large internet companies and their large data sets. Indeed, the phrase *big data*, often associated with AI, suggests that using proprietary data sets to leverage AI in building great experiences is a unique opportunity limited to the largest internet companies. In my experience, that could not be further from the truth. Across the Bloomreach customer base—ranging from medium- and large-scale retailers to banks, health care organizations, governments, and business-to-business companies—data is rarely the limiter. In fact, there are very few of those businesses that fully leverage their data to maximize its potential. More often, the existence of good-quality data infrastructure, a team that knows what to do with it, and a clear point of view on how that data can be harnessed to affect business outcomes are the limiters.

What's next for AI? So far, work in AI has been focused on recognition and understanding. The future breakthroughs will be in AI creation: the point at which an AI bot will make a phone call rather than just responding to speech or text. This creation is still in its early phases: We can't yet create undetectable "deep fakes" of videos and photographs. And we have yet to see a computer compose extraordinary music. But this is the direction of AI, and experts in the field have high hopes. The YouTube cats are only the beginning, they say. "We went from completely subhuman to equal to a human to now completely superhuman because somehow now computers with a few pixels of a lemon peel can identify that that's a picture of a lemon—something a human is never going to be able to do," says Srinath Sridhar. "Now the future seems to be that in some aspects computers will be superhuman in text, speech and vision."

We continue to see AI systems evolve to be able to make more and more sense of the world around us and to do that with less and less expertise-driven training. The promise of AI is that it may have the potential to really understand what we are seeking—to interpret our actions, our speech, our clicks, our emotions, our relationships, indeed our whole being; to identify what we are seeking and figure out how to give it to each of us.

AMBIENT

While AI grabs the headlines, another technology trend folds into this story, and that is what we call ambient technologies—mobile, voice, sensors, wearables, drones, and all kinds of computing every-where that enable us to get a more complete picture of our seeker. We understand human beings much more deeply—capturing their every movement, every click, every speech, and even every breath. A little scary? Yes, but also exciting. For the first time, ambient tech-nologies give us a shot at not just understanding what our customer is telling us but also getting to what they may be truly seeking. All the signals captured by ambient interfaces then feed our massive AI-powered brain, which can crunch those thousands of signals to make sense of them. Is our customer heading to work in their car today and interested in being briefed on work items or heading to a loved one's house and in need of the perfect gift? AI can tell us it's the latter, but the data inputs come from ambient technologies.

Ambient technology represents a giant leap beyond the type of search activity we might have conducted at our desktops back in the first generation. "Suppose you are driving and your tire pressure light comes on. What do you do?" asks Ravi N. Raj, a former Bloomreach head of product and CEO of Passage AI, which he recently sold to

ServiceNow. "The ten blue links of a desktop search don't really work. Suppose you could ask the car what to do next. And instead of ten blue links to the owner's manual, it says: 'The front tire pressure should be set at 28 psi.' " You've moved from searching to providing the right answer—in your car.

This kind of conversational AI has transformed computing and communications, typically manifesting in two primary ways: voice and chat. The emergence of voice assistants—Amazon Echo, Google Home, and Apple Siri—has taken a serial interface, voice, and made it the kind of interactive ever-present computing device that neatly folds into the background of our home or phone. Initially we assumed we would be asking our voice assistants the same thing we may type into a search box. But our behavior with a "typed search query" has diverged quite a bit from our use of those assistants. Google Trends reports that the top searches on Google in 2019 in the United States included "Disney Plus," "Cameron Boyce," "Nipsey Hustle," "Hurricane Dorian," and "Antonio Brown." These are all classic informational queries. On the other hand, CNBC reports that three of the top uses of smart speakers are "playing music or the radio," "playing audiobooks or podcasts," and "making purchases" (which a remarkable 7 percent of people do). All three of these involve a person commanding the speaker to do something rather than asking for information.

The stark contrast reveals a deep truth about ambient technologies: they typically augment our understanding of the user rather than simply replacing a pattern of interaction that may occur on more traditional computing platforms like phones or computers.

Ravi took on another conversational interface that has exploded in recent years—chat. Chat is not new to the Web. But it certainly has exploded. Facebook Messenger now has 1.2 billion users, Whatsapp (also owned by Facebook) has 1.8 billion users, and WeChat dominates Chinese chat, with 1.4 billion users. Where voice and video can provide rich, fulsome interactions, chat excels at providing efficient communications for multitaskers. Indeed, most millennials report that they much prefer to have communicate with them through text or chat rather than voice calls. Ravi has taken the concept of conversational interfaces and extended it with AI and natural language processing. The results permit the creation of unique seeker-centric experiences. He describes an example with tiremaker Bridgestone, which operates a network of dealerships across the world. Because of its use of Passage AI, you can interact directly with an AI-powered chatbot to diagnose low tire pressure, identify a nearby dealership, make an appointment, and perhaps share the details of the car that you're bringing in. And you can do all this without interacting with a human being. Like their voice-based counterparts, chatbots permit us to more deeply understand the underlying intent of our customers. A Bridgestone dealer has the opportunity to know, before you show up at the dealership, that you're coming in for a tire replacement for a particular car at a particular time and can be ready to serve you.

Ambient interfaces do not stop with voice and chat. We are surrounded by them: smart ovens, smart televisions, Nest thermostats, and smart alarms. We wear them for our fitness needs in the form of smart watches and Fitbits. Our clothing increasingly consists of wearables. Interestingly, wearables open up a typically less technologically inclined demographic—adults over sixty-five years old, whose natural focus on their health has driven adoption. Each of these ambient devices transmits a constant stream of data about us to smart systems in the cloud. Indeed, ambient interfaces enable us to take a leap forward in understanding our customers' underlying intentions, needs, and desires.

A terrific example of an increasingly ambient device is the drone. It has at its core a set of cameras and environmental sensors. While drones as Christmas gifts may be sources of entertainment, they are increasingly doing serious business and showing the power of these ambient interfaces in a range of industrial applications.

George Mathew has been a multiple-time entrepreneur in Silicon Valley, and his most recent venture is Kespry, which uses drones to power industrial applications. Many of Kespry's largest deployments involve gathering information from some of the less accessible places in the world. Its drones might, for example, collect data around oil and gas refineries to understand the condition of the assets that may be present there. George tells a personal story of his experience during Hurricane Harvey in Texas. He explains that in the aftermath of the storm, there was a high demand for insurance adjusters to climb on roofs to assess damages. It turns out that roofing is the third most dangerous profession in the United States. On top of that, demand for adjusters at insurance companies skyrocketed, resulting in long waits for settlements. Drone-based surveying enabled insurance companies to complete their assessments more quickly, more accurately, and more safely than by sending people to go climb on roofs. George describes the evolution of drones from "novelty to the new normal."

While the first applications of drones may involve gathering information and data, an even more powerful application is within reach. Ambient interfaces don't just listen to us; they can do things for us. Enter drone delivery.

Several years ago drone delivery of packages seemed like an Amazon PR stunt. Several years later it is very real. My friend Faisal Masud spent much of his career turning around and growing digital businesses at Amazon, eBay, and Staples. He recently served as the chief operating officer and adviser to Google/Alphabet's Wing project, which focuses on drone-based delivery of freight. Wing has completed over eighty thousand deliveries at its test sites in the United States and Australia. It has recently partnered with FedEx and Walgreens to begin autonomous drone delivery of packages in the United States. While the trials are early, the impact could be profound. Faisal believes that the initial applications of drone delivery will be in semirural areas, where distances mean that same-day (or -hour) shipping can be challenging. The initial set of goods, as indicated by Walgreens, will typically involve staples—basic groceries and medicines. It might feel like the march from three-day to two-day to same-day shipping seems unnecessary for most situations. Who exactly needs the same-hour delivery that drones permit? For a new mom looking for formula for a newborn who's crying, the goal is to satisfy her infant immediately. Same-hour delivery might be too slow. Like with all new technologies, we pattern our acceptance after the people around us. When the new normal is watching our neighbor get a package within the hour, drones may become the primary way we get the things we order online.

Ambient interfaces are exactly that—ambient. They fade into the background if they are doing their jobs right. While the first-generation Web needed us to tell it what we wanted, the ambient world can hazard a very good guess. These interfaces are a source of data for intelligent systems in the cloud and for ever-present computing devices taking actions that satisfy our most immediate needs.

In fact, Xun Wang, Bloomreach's chief technology officer, predicts even more computing power will be moving into these kinds of edge ambient devices. Whereas a lot of today's ambient devices simply send back data to the mothership for processing and sense-making, Xun sees the power of the data center throughout the thirty devices connected to the Web in his living room. He sees the pendulum shifting somewhat back from centralized computing to grids of computing power at the edge. As that pendulum shifts, the amount of passive computing (computing done without any explicit instruction from us) will continue to dwarf the active computing (where we sit in front of a device and work with it). It seems likely that just as we no longer worry about the capacity on our email account, cameras in the ambient interfaces all around us will be capturing our interactions, not waiting for us to take a picture. Perhaps the ambient interfaces won't just be listening to us and doing things for us; they will themselves be a bigger part of our networked and AI-driven brain power.

APIs

And now our final A—APIs. They are an outgrowth of service-oriented computing—the basic notion being that any piece of digital business logic can be wrapped in such a way that a consumer of that service does not need to know how it was built. This means a third party can simply use it without understanding it. It is the digital equivalent of the supply chain: just as the automaker can simply buy a tire in the digital world in order to make a car, a retailer might be able to lend money by calling a lending "service" from a bank or credit check organization via API. Neither the automaker nor the retailer needs to know how the tire or the lending service is made. They can buy it and put it into service for their own customers without having to learn that particular process themselves.

APIs have taken off in the last ten years, making it a great time to be a developer. The prevalence of APIs has unleashed the creativity of their users. We used to think of AI and ML as something that required a degree in rocket surgery in order to be successful and right. Today you can tap AWS's AI and ML services from Microsoft or Google. APIs today can make anybody successful regardless of their level of experience. Users have access to more capabilities. They can take the existing components that were developed by rocket scientists and assemble them to do something that's completely original.

But where did this all come from? In many ways, the commercial open-source model was the forefather of today's cloud-based APIs. With the emergence of open source projects, developers could collaborate across the world to build great software. Other builders of software could then take open source libraries and embed them in their own creations—compounding the rate of innovation. In the days of early open-source projects, while the software might be crowdsourced, the infrastructure was not. As a developer, you still had to deal with bringing up servers, storage, and other infrastructure. You still had to ensure that the code was written in the appropriate language and was compatible with the operating system you were using. While the software around open source may have been free, everything it took to bring it to life was not—hence, the development of commercial open source. Nonetheless, the open source revolution did promote the idea that highly specialized groups of developers could build unique technology that others could use in their pursuits. In fact, early open-source libraries contained early forms of APIs. But ultimately APIs would really come to life only with the emergence of the clouds because they fundamentally changed the affordability and accessibility of third-party services that were delivered via API. To use an analogy, the API is a lot like the standards that ensure phone networks can communicate with each other regardless of the country they operate in, so we can make a call anywhere in the world. But until the cost of the phone comes down, making it affordable, the power of that network will be constrained.

AWS is often credited as the original API-driven cloud. It launched in 2006 with three core services: Simple Storage Service (S3), Elastic Compute Cloud (EC2), and Simple Queue Service (SQS). The key was the word *simple*. AWS did not aim to create complex services for every need. Instead, it aimed to create a minimum viable product—the simplest utility service it could create, wrapped with the simplest APIs possible, for maximum scalability. Like any good Lego block maker, AWS believed it was more important to create highly reusable Lego blocks and to leave the building to the imagination of the builders rather than envisioning every possible use and complicating the blocks. A decade and a half later the quantity, quality, reach, and scale of those APIs have exploded. Like in any robust market, Amazon is not alone. Microsoft's Azure and GCP have joined it as preeminent public clouds. Large software vendors like Salesforce, Oracle, IBM, and Adobe have their own clouds, many of which enable enterprises to build their own private clouds and specialized vertical or functional applications. The pay-per-use business model that public cloud vendors pioneered also meant that the consumers of the API would pay more as their application got more and more use. In effect, it was like paying for the building blocks based on how many people visited the building. At the core of the scalability of the cloud services has been the API, an abstraction layer that ensured that the consumer of any service, no matter how complex, could avoid worrying about the complexity behind the service interface and simply know they could reliably build on it.

Behind the API revolution, software itself has become increasingly specialized, forming a series of microservices—while the API may be the wrapper, inside each wrapper is a self-contained unit, a service, that is focused on what it does and can communicate with other services via APIs. Microservices and APIs are not just for public clouds. In every major enterprise technology stack, IT organizations are building microservices and disaggregating their monolithic applications. Whether or not they ultimately choose to expose these services externally, even internal applications benefit from the reusability and accessibility of APIs.

In the years since the launch of AWS, a lot has changed. The APIs themselves have become more and more standardized, using a paradigm that developers describe as *RESTful*—a simple request/response paradigm that eases both development and consumption. APIs also keep moving "up the stack." While the early APIs were limited to infrastructure building blocks like computing and storage, we now have everything from image recognition APIs to email delivery APIs and even vertical applications delivered via API. In fact, Bloomreach is itself an example of an "up the stack" collection of cloud-based APIs. By offering APIs for merchandising, search, search engine optimization, analytics, content management, and personalization, Bloomreach represents a collection of everything a digital experience builder needs to create a world-class experience, powered by world-class AI.

As APIs become richer and more vertical centric, they become more and more applicable to real-world problems. In the past, building an e-commerce experience required spending millions of dollars on an e-commerce platform from IBM or Oracle or Salesforce and then spending millions more on Accenture consultants to stand up a high-quality enterprise commerce experience. All that could take a year or two. It then required hiring an army of people to operate and optimize the software. With clouds and APIs, everything is different. A small brand can sign up on Shopify and have a robust storefront in days. A larger company can partner with Bloomreach and a range of our modern commerce partners—commercetools, Elastic Path, and Big Commerce—to launch a commerce experience on any channel for a fraction of the cost and within weeks. A core effect of the emergence of cloud-based APIs is the dramatic impact on developer velocity, allowing an order-of-magnitude reduction in the time and money needed to build something. Perhaps equally important, the standardization of APIs has meant that the expertise needed for developers has continued to decrease. The earliest APIs still required the developer to understand them deeply—or at least to understand the environment in which they were going to be deployed. They required the developer to recompile their applications and engendered specialized roles. Today consuming APIs requires only the most basic computer science training. The upgrading of APIs to add more and more value with higher and higher levels of abstraction has only accelerated in recent years. It started by abstracting the hardware elements (computing and storage resources), moved to partitioning servers (virtualization), and proceeded to abstracting operating systems (containers), capacity and scaling (serverless), and algorithms (ML and AI).

The emergence of APIs as a paradigm has ultimately created a high degree of technology specialization with significant business impacts. We see that clearly in the nature of legacy platforms used to build e-commerce sites. Legacy platforms have historically had an all-in-one mindset. A platform like Salesforce's Commerce Cloud for consumer-facing businesses (Demandware) includes an unholy marriage of everything from shopping cart software to shipping, logistics, search, page creation, and so many more elements. The trouble is that none of them is best in class. The API mindset forces each provider of an API to ask "Is my service the best in the world?" Because as easy as it is to connect to an API, it is equally easy to disconnect from it.

As the API economy has grown, sorting through it takes more time and effort. Like anything else, with high demand and reduced cost comes a proliferation of services of varying applicability and quality. And while the individual services have become more powerful, picking the right ones for the given purpose and putting them together while ensuring they meet performance, cost, and security objectives requires increasing knowledge and expertise.

But why does the proliferation of APIs matter to building seeker-centric, winning experiences? Remember, at the core of our seekers is a desire to solve problems and get to the higher-order intention of the human being. While the customer might look for a plane ticket, the seeker is looking for a memorable family vacation. Reliably delivering a flight reservation is a massively less complex task than delivering a memorable family vacation, which requires coordination among services delivered by an airline, a travel agent, a reviews website, the family photos, the location of the travelers, the age of the kids, and so much more. How can one organization build all this? It can't. And that's where the API economy comes in. The promise of APIs is that they will allow each of the service providers to specialize but will enable an aggregator to call on all those services in real time to deliver the memorable vacation. APIs are computing's equivalent of the comparative advantages that are at the heart of our free-trade economic system. Each provider can be best in class at what it does, and each consumer can benefit from the assembly of those services to meet their goals.

APIs have become increasingly important in a mobile era. Digital experiences of the past primarily meant websites. But a lot has changed. Today the average consumer has at least thirteen interactions with a brand before transacting with it. Some of those interactions are physical. Some are via email. Others are on a website or mobile application. Some might be via the ambient technologies—chat or voice. How does a brand ensure that the communication with the seeker is relevant and coordinated across all those different interaction points? APIs are key to making that possible.

The power of cloud-based APIs in our tale doesn't stop at the sum of their parts. As Xun went from developing PC-based gaming software to cloud-based gaming software, he saw an era of games that weren't just cheaper or faster to produce but that simply could not have existed in a previous era. Games like Fortnight, multiplayer in nature with incredible graphics, could never have been rendered on older devices. Imagine the example of a developer who wants to build an interactive video shopping experience. APIs from the large clouds could be used to understand the images, extracting products out of them; APIs from Bloomreach could be used to recommend similar products; and APIs from still others could be used to understand the sentiment or reaction of the shopper to the recommendation. The whole is much greater than the sum of the parts.

INTERSECTIONS

Each of the three As has reinforcing effects on the others. For example, a smart thermostat might be able to regulate heat in a house, but when that data goes back to the cloud, networked across multiple homes and optimized for demand by AI, the overall grid becomes smarter and more efficient. Like most technology trends, they build on each other, forming an edifice that transforms our digital lives. None of the technologies I've described is especially new. AI and neural networks have been talked about at computer science conferences for decades. Sensors have been used in certain industrial applications for an equally long time. And earlier forms of APIs have existed in PC-based computing for many years. But a lot has changed in the last decade as AI-based applications became production worthy, ambient devices started to rapidly proliferate, and public cloud–based APIs became the primary Lego blocks of most web-based applications. Together they form the basis of a new kind of platform, a digital experience platform, that is at the heart of winning digital experiences.

Before these technology trends, it was natural that we would think of the customer and not deeply understand or be able to react to the higher-order intentions of the seeker. The primary internet collection devices have been the computer and the phone—and our primary input mechanisms have been clicks, swipes, and character strokes on a keyboard. Each of these data inputs is explicit: I dictate the information I share with a website or application explicitly so it knows only what I want it to know. But ambient technology changes all that; it turns the environment around us into a continuous observation deck, collecting not just what we explicitly share but also what we implicitly share, thereby forming a fuller picture of who we are and what we seek. In a pre-AI world, human analysis of data was the best avenue we had to make sense of what we knew. That process was inevitably slow, incomplete, and unable to process information at large scale. But AI has changed all that. Because of AI, we are able to make sense of massive amounts of data and respond in real time. Importantly to the seeker revolution, we can use deep-learning techniques to piece together ostensibly unrelated signals and understand the true motivations of the seeker. Finally, in a pre-cloud API era, businesses would have had to take on the daunting burden of building highly complicated digital experiences, often requiring competencies and capital that were unrealistic. Now we can assemble the products and services the seeker is seeking, benefiting from the specialization of microservices all around us.

Ambient technology listens to the seeker, AI unlocks true seeker intent, APIs enable the assembly of the perfect experience, and we return to ambient devices to deliver it. The perfect storm of technology generates the winning experience.

5

BUILD YOUR DIGITAL DREAMS; DON'T BUY THEM

Acronyms are the bread and butter of Silicon Valley—ERP, CRM, CDP, CMS, etc. We use them because we are taught that great businesses are built with category leadership and that so many category leaders pioneered the category they later led. Salesforce pioneered the software-as-a-service category and made the acronym SAAS synonymous with the modern delivery of software, where customers don't need to install the software on their machines and they are assured access to the right version of the software without painful upgrades. Unfortunately, the acronym soup that technology companies have created, while intended to put descriptors on things, often creates more noise than clarity. In the middle of all that noise, it can be hard to parse out which acronyms are marketing gimmicks and which ones represent profound transformations in technology that have significant business impact.

One of those acronyms, DXP, or digital experience platform, has emerged as among the most powerful trends in the modern Web. I had no idea what a DXP was or should be when I started Bloomreach, but I have come to embrace it as a strategy for winning digital experiences. In particular, I have come to understand that e-commerce, where so many digital trends take root, needs a DXP specifically built for commerce.

When I started out in 2010, the goal was straightforward: build a more relevant experience so that when you and I visited websites, we found what we were looking for, with minimal effort or friction. As I double-clicked on so many of those websites, I discovered a pretty straightforward problem. There was way too much content and way too many visitors to large websites for a one-size-fits-all experience to work. To make matters worse, websites were (and often still are) manually curated—basically they change at the rate a human being can identify the need for a change and make it. Ultimately, there was no hope of building a better Web if our websites couldn't get better while we were sleeping at night, learning from every individual click and nonclick. That realization led me to start Bloomreach, recruiting a team of people who had built search at Google to invert the problem. Instead of building a pure search engine where someone would type in a phrase and the search engine would crawl the Web and return the most relevant results it could find, why couldn't all the websites in the world know what the user was seeking and show them exactly what they were looking for when they got there? Ten years later I realized that the platform we built represents a DXP, and every significant digital business needs one.

Gartner describes a DXP as "an integrated and cohesive piece of technology designed to enable the composition, management, delivery and optimization of contextualized digital experiences across multi-experience customer journeys." Whoa! Now that's a mouthful. Put simply, as the customer seeks deeper and deeper engagement and has higher and higher expectations, digital brands need to keep up. They need technology to speak to those individuals in a highly relevant manner—at all times. Perhaps that is a simple problem, but it is easier said than done.

The era of seeker-centric digital business has also driven a complete transformation in the technology stack that businesses need to compete in a digital world. At its core, businesses have moved their websites, apps, and other owned digital experiences from an application to a platform. In the old days, you bought application software to help publish a website. As a larger business, you used an e-commerce system (like Salesforce Commerce Cloud or Oracle Commerce) or a content management system (like Adobe's suite of tools) to publish a website. As a smaller business, you used tools like Wordpress or Hubspot or Shopify. That suite of tools was perfectly suited for the era of digital marketing. The job of those platforms was pretty straightforward: help my marketing team build websites and run digital marketing campaigns, primarily on Google and Facebook, to communicate with my customers. No wonder everyone's website looked the same and did the same thing.

The trouble is this: If you build a digital experience that looks and feels the same to every consumer, why won't they just go to Amazon?

Indeed, great digital businesses are built, not bought. They need digital teams to dream up the Symptom Checker like the National Health Service did or pilot video tagging driven by artificial intelligence (AI) like the United States Tennis Association did or provide unique promotions of own-brand products like Staples has. If you've defined your offering appropriately, your seeker is unique to you. While Tesla and Mercedes may both produce electric-powered vehicles, the center of each of their bull's-eyes represents unique seekers, and they can both win by building the perfect vehicle for their specific group. The best way to stand out is to understand what you do uniquely for your seeker and build it. That needs a completely different technology set—one that allows you to put in your unique IP and unique brand. It needs a platform, not an application.

Today digital experiences have crossed from digital marketing to digital business, necessitating a DXP for every major company doing business digitally—which is every major company. I see that throughout the many experiences being built on our and other platforms. Hilton Hotels runs core online reservations on our platform. ING Group runs online banking on our DXP. Neiman Marcus runs much of its e-commerce on our platform. None of these large global brands sees its digital presence as a marketing shingle. That presence is unmistakably woven into the fabric of the organization and how it speaks to, serves, and makes money from their customers. The transition from digital marketing to digital business profoundly changes everything about how organizations approach digital. To start with, digital is no longer the job of the chief marketing officer. It has ushered in roles like the chief digital officer and a whole team of digital experts.

While the word *platform* is among the most overused pieces of the technology lexicon, in this case it is totally accurate. We can think of the new role of the digital team as that of a team of digital business builders with a clearly identified seeker at the center and a desire to build a highly unique experience that speaks to them. What they build needs to be comprehensive—driven by product managers who define the experience, designers who design it, developers who write software to develop it, information security architects who secure it, digital marketers who market it, sellers who sell it, and executives who drive an end-to-end business around it. The digital experience platform is the canvas on which all those roles can collaborate and build together.

COMPONENTS OF A WINNING DXP

The core of a modern DXP is a giant matching engine. Thousands, hundreds of thousands, or millions of people may be visiting your digital experience. You've spent a huge amount of time and money getting them there. What do you show them in the moment of truth? At any reasonable scale, it would be impossible for a human being to manually select a given piece of content or a product or service to offer. Rather, your platform needs to crunch through all the products, services, or pieces of content and match them to your seeker. To do all that, it needs to first understand what your seeker seeks (demand) and then understand what you offer (supply). At the scale of even a medium-sized commerce business, that means understanding the motivations of millions of consumers and the details of hundreds of

Figure 5.1 The DXP is made up of several seeker-centric components.

thousands of products. Therefore, at the core of your DXP must be a strong foundation in data. The data typically comes in five forms:

- Product data: The products you offer and their attributes (for example, a lamp can be of various sizes, types, or makes);
- Content data: Typically the articles, videos, and images that describe your offering;
- Marketing data: The campaigns, creatives, email lists, mobile numbers, and other data you may use in your digital marketing programs;
- Interaction data: The various clicks, swipes, email opens, views, locations, and other ambient data about your seeker; and
- Transactional data: The past purchases or transactions your seeker may have made.

In order to understand your seeker and respond to them with the right offering at the right time, you have to deeply understand them (interactions and transactions) and deeply understand your own assets (products, content, and marketing). Having a core mechanism to ingest and understand these varying types of data distinguishes a modern DXP from its predecessors.

Once the data comes into the system, the job of the DXP is to make sense of it. That's where AI comes in. Older DXPs will largely provide manual mechanisms for marketers and merchandisers to use to do the sense-making. Modern DXPs will come with built-in algorithms. These algorithms, backed by best-in-class AI, are of four core types:

- Personalization: These algorithms understand the seeker and ensure that the offerings you put in front of them represent your best understanding of their current intent. Personalization algorithms ensure that each of us gets our unique experience.
- Relevance: Such algorithms take what the seeker explicitly expresses, perhaps by entering something in a search box or by scrolling through your app, and ensure that the right offering is presented to them. Relevance algorithms ensure everyone has a baseline relevant experience.
- Business optimization: What if you offer different types of sweaters and they are all a good match for the seeker? Business optimization algorithms will rightly display the sweater that maximizes revenue, profits, or some other business goal for your digital business.
- Marketing optimization: Digital experiences are certainly about the experience, but they are also marketing vehicles that we run our campaigns against. Marketing optimization algorithms ensure that we show up in search engines, social media feeds, email messages, and other marketing tactics.

Algorithms and AI are necessary but not sufficient capabilities of a great platform. So much of business is specific—and increasingly so in a seeker-centric world. There is not one strategy that wins in banking or health care or retail—there are many. And as we discussed earlier, the DXP is a canvas. The true authors are the marketers and merchandisers whose individual business insights must be reflected in the brand's digital experiences. At a home improvement business like Home Depot, this may mean ensuring customers can stitch together an experience that involves both content around "how to build a deck" and the associated products and services that may help them do it. At a B2B business like HD Supply, it may mean understanding which parts are being reordered often so these can be proactively stocked in the supply chain. Each of these business processes is unique, and as digital experts move away from the job of keeping websites operational (because technology should take care of that part), they still need a way to curate, personalize, and optimize experiences based on their unique job functions and business priorities.

To help the digital experts accomplish that goal, a DXP should come with the right combination of tools and dashboards, including

- Channel management: The ability to manage multiple channels—various websites, mobile applications, voice interfaces, or other customer-facing channels;
- Digital merchandising: The ability to take products and services and display them in the way that most effectively drives outcomes;
- Content management: The ability to edit, manage, preview, version, and otherwise manage the content elements of an experience;
- Recommendations: The ability to build unique personalized recommendations so that various cohorts of customers can benefit from the wisdom of similar users or buyers;
- Search management: The ability to manage the search capabilities to assure that the most relevant content or products match what the user is looking for;
- Insights: The ability to deeply understand customers, products, and content elements to continuously recommend how experiences might improve; and
- Testing and targeting: The ability to select specific groups of customers, offer uniquely targeted content or products to them, and then test against the target key performance indicators and iterate toward better results.

Great tools and an amazing AI engine enable the generation of a great experience, but there is a key element of a DXP that is essential to capture the breadth of ambient interactions that seekers seek— application program interfaces (APIs) in the cloud. As our seekers move among email, text and mobile applications, and more, we need a way to integrate their interaction mode of choice, assuring that the right experience is presented to them at the right time. The key to that is a collection of APIs that any developer can connect to their front-end application. Therefore, a great DXP offers a robust collection of APIs, including APIs for content, content metadata, categories and filters, products, search, recommendations, and search engine optimization (SEO). APIs enable a DXP to be consumed modularly. We see the power of APIs across a wide variety of Bloomreach clients. One of our customers, Staples, which is a leader in the business-to-business (B2B) and consumer office supplies area, started by using our SEO API to drive better customer acquisition to their properties. Then they moved to our search and categories APIs, as they wanted AI-enabled search and browse functions for their digital experiences. Finally, they leveraged our content APIs to begin to build whole experiences on the platform—content and commerce. The journey that Staples took—across the services Bloomreach offered them and across various brands, businesses, and countries—was not unique. The days of big bang projects that cost tens of millions of dollars are behind us; leading digital businesses want to work iteratively to deliver what the seeker seeks.

Finally, a great DXP should offer a wide range of flexible "front ends" or accelerators so that businesses can get up and running quickly. In e-commerce, that may include consumer-focused store-fronts that developers can use to quickly stand up their commerce experience. In B2B, that may include key components like reordering and other service functionalities so businesses can take advantage of customer service online. In health care, that may include HIPAA-compliant authentication or General Data Protection Regulation support to handle data and patient privacy. Increasingly we see accelerators that take advantage of client-side technologies based on Javascript like React, Angular, and Vue. These client-side technologies provide seekers with a far more interactive and immersive experience, making websites feel more and more like mobile applications. It also means that developers of digital experiences no longer need to be experts in Java or other server-side programming languages. Java developers are hard to find, and building great Java applications takes time and money. Instead, a front-end developer can load an accelerator, focus on building a modern digital experience, and rely on all the back-end APIs provided for in the DXP to do the heavy lifting of creating an AI-enabled experience—all while being assured that the full complement of curation tools will be available to their business counterparts if they wish to edit or manage anything.

OPEN FOR BUSINESS

Platforms, while good business for software companies, have come to be understood by CIOs as locking companies into proprietary stacks. Ask so many technology leaders, and their reaction to buying a new platform is akin to our reaction when we have to buy the new Apple headphone or charger that works only with Apple devices—dismay and skepticism. Those concerns are not just real but also substantial inhibitors to success in a rapidly evolving and heterogeneous digital environment. Your average enterprise has seventeen different content management systems and an equally fragmented environment for customer data, for marketing systems, and for everything else. Often the technology was selected by predecessors. Sometimes it comes in through acquisition. Either way, dealing with heterogeneity is the norm, not the exception.

That is why a modern DXP must be open. The dream of buying every piece of software from a single vendor and having "one throat to choke" no longer feels realistic. The world is moving too fast, and we must be responsive to the seeker without being burdened by technology religion. While DXPs should come with prebuilt capabilities like the ones outlined above, they must also be open for business and easily integrate into a wide variety of systems and data sources. Openness comes in a number of core forms:

- Data: A good DXP should be able to ingest and expose the core data elements in its platform—enabling customer or marketing or product data to flow in and out. We see a digital brand like Albertsons (which owns Safeway) provide Bloomreach with data around the past purchases of its customers to enable seekers to digitally build grocery lists without the need to remember what they bought last time.
- Algorithms: World-class DXPs should enable algorithms to be customized—maintaining best-in-class AI but training on models that benefit from different data sets, different weights, and different inputs and that are optimized against different goals. We see large fashion retailers like Next PLC provide forecasts of new products that they are pioneering so their partners' algorithms can optimize against not only past performance but also future forecasts.
- Dashboards and tools: We discussed earlier in this chapter how important it was to offer robust dashboards and tools for marketers and merchandisers. But what if those marketers need capabilities not offered in the platform? An open dashboard or tools infrastructure would permit developers to add Open UI components so that third-party capabilities would be visible in the platform. We have seen partners easily add SEO modules and digital asset management capabilities to the Bloomreach DXP.
- Components: Digital experiences are inherently collections of components and services displayed to seekers to help them accomplish their goals. Every experience is built on a collection of components. At its simplest level, those components might be banners, content elements, templates, videos, and products. But in a modern digital experience, dynamic components like login, reorder, search, and so many others also represent components. No DXP stack can offer every component you may need one day. Therefore, component development must be open and democratized. We have seen partners like the Born Group, a leading digital agency, build its own collection of components for specific vertical applications.

- Connectors: Finally, digital experiences need to connect to different systems—perhaps Marketo for campaign management or Salesforce for customer relations management (CRM) or SAP for transactional commerce. A great DXP should offer the ability to connect to any third-party system so that data and communication can flow between them.

NOT YOUR MOTHER'S E-COMMERCE STOREFRONT

I met Dirk Hoerig, the founder of commercetools, through our mutual participation in various commerce conferences. I was speaking to the emergence of a new kind of digital experience, and Dirk was evangelizing about a concept that has come to be known as headless commerce. Dirk had spent much of his working life in Munich, Germany, building a small agency that specialized in one of the world's largest commerce platforms—Hybris. Hybris (now SAP Hybris) was a pioneering e-commerce technology that today powers some of the largest e-commerce environments in the world. It started in Europe and, on the strength of its capabilities in product catalog management, became the platform of choice for some of the most complex commerce environments, many in the B2B space that needed to cater to businesses with very unique requirements. Dirk's agency grew on the back of Hybris, and he launched some of the early e-commerce storefronts for great brands like Puma. As he was deploying and building on the Hybris software, he came to a couple of key realizations. It was taking huge amounts of time and money to deploy, scale, and version the software. He watched Marc Benioff take CRM to the cloud at Salesforce and resolved to do something similar in commerce: to build the kind of commerce system that had all the flexibility that Hybris had but none of the headaches that come with deploying infrastructure and upgrading versions. Dirk's second realization was that the level of customization needed to power great experiences was only going to increase as people started transacting in different countries, with different currencies, with unique promotional logic, and with unique product catalogs.

He resolved that developers needed to be able to customize their commerce back end.

Finally he observed that e-commerce in the future was going to be multichannel. He remembers reading the *Wired* article that Chris Anderson wrote in 2010 titled "The Web Is Dead." When you turned the page, you got the shocking follow-on: "Long Live the Internet." Indeed, he felt a commerce platform must support a core set of APIs that developers could use to power experiences outside of the website. Out of those core realizations came the idea of a headless commerce platform: a platform that includes a core set of capabilities to power catalogs, payments, carts, authentication, promotion, and so many other services but not the core customer experience or front end. The headless commerce engine assumes that someone else will build the user experience on top of a platform—breaking the tight coupling that SAP Hybris, Oracle Commerce, Salesforce Commerce, and so many other leading commerce platforms had built on. Indeed, commercetools would specialize in everything that comes after a user hits "Add to cart" and leave the rest to an experience platform that was really good at its job rather than promoting the unholy marriage between transactional commerce capabilities and experience capabilities.

In North America, companies like Elastic Path and Big Commerce were charting similar paths, and headless commerce has become the hottest trend in digital commerce as leaders like SAP and Salesforce invest to catch up with the early winners.

Dirk observes that so many of his customers are really building tech companies of their own, with hundreds of developers building unique commerce experiences. They run agile development processes and think of themselves as product organizations. He talks about Lego.com, which views its digital experience not just as websites and apps but as creating a unique customer experience across any touchpoint. Another example Dirk refers to is Volkswagen where the digital shopping experience crosses multiple boundaries— from online car configuration to in-car commerce. The shopper of the future is connected with the products and services they use.

The key insight here is that e-commerce is no longer a monolith. Rather, with the emergence of headless commerce, we have broken it up between the transactional back-end set of services (a stable set of capabilities to handle transactions and business processes) and an experience front-end set of services (everything that you present to your users and customers). Both are collections of APIs that run in the cloud, but where your headless commerce engine specializes in processing the order, your experience platform specializes in getting the customer engaged in your offering deeply enough to buy. At the lower end of the market, platforms like Shopify will continue to offer one-size-fits-all capabilities to quickly stand up a basic storefront. But as businesses mature, they will seek to convey their unique competitive advantage online. When they get there, they will not want their storefront to look and feel like those of all their competitors. They will want the agility, flexibility, and optimization of an AI-driven DXP, purpose built for e-commerce, coupled with a strong set of headless commerce capabilities to process the order.

At Bloomreach, we see several digital organizations double down on the headless commerce + DXP trend. Customers like Paige, which sells designer jeans, evaluated whether to run their digital experience completely on Salesforce Commerce Cloud and decided that a modern technology stack like Bloomreach + commercetools gave them the agility they needed to distinguish themselves with their seeker. They were rewarded for their choice: they gained all the AI-driven benefits of a modern DXP, full experiential control, and the ability to stand up a storefront in sixty days—all for a few hundred thousand dollars. A similar project with a more traditional platform choice would have taken years, yielded much less in terms of revenue growth, and cost millions of dollars. Gaming brand Pokémon made a similar decision with Bloomreach + Elastic Path. Others have chosen Bloomreach + Big Commerce. Headless commerce is in its infancy, but it's certainly coming.

Commerce is the tip of the spear for the DXP to take hold in the market. It has all the ingredients of a market in transition: a disruptive competitive threat (Amazon), a strong economic motivation to drive more customers and more conversion (revenue growth), and a seeker who will switch unless you serve them uniquely. No longer does a commerce business need to invest millions of dollars in consulting or systems to build a great experience. If it is happy with its current transactional commerce stack (as so many are), it simply consumes better search, better personalization, and better content management via API and offers a great experience. If the company is launching a new experience, it picks a headless commerce engine, couples that with its experience platform, and gets started innovating.

These key ingredients have led commerce experience stacks to be among the first to adopt the winner's technology stack. We should expect that commerce is the canary in the coal mine. We see the new experience stacks taking hold in a wide range of other Bloomreach clients. ING Group is rolling out its DXP across online banking. Capital One is offering unique digital financial services. And our friends at the NHS continue to think about how to build the digital stack of the future for health care.

BUILD VERSUS BUY

Thinking through how a commerce business should pick its platform led me to a conversation with Brian Walker, who serves as chief strategy officer of Bloomreach after prior stints at Amazon, Accenture, SAP Hybris, and Forrester Research. Brian pioneered the concept of the commerce platform while at Forrester. He thinks about the commerce stack strategy of businesses on a digital maturity curve—with organizations that are early to the Web relying on all-in-one platforms like a Shopify (for small businesses) or an Adobe (for large businesses) and those that are at scale and looking to innovate and differentiate gravitating to the DXP paradigm.

But if we are talking about businesses looking to build experiences, why do they need a platform at all? Why not build it all? Brian tells the story of Blue Apron, which had built a whole host of software to accommodate the very unique business challenge of meal delivery. The trouble was that it was rebuilding a bunch of capabilities that already existed in the world, built with higher quality by firms that specialized in them. Tens of millions of dollars of technology investment later, the company struggled to find a way out. At Bloomreach, we see a similar dynamic with some of the largest businesses that seek to build their own search engine. After investing tens of millions of dollars in building, they buy that service from us. The takeaway from build versus buy is not to never build; it is to build the right things. Building software is a specialized task, needing specialized people and a long-term investment horizon. It is important to build the things that set you apart and ensure your platform choice supports the rest.

THE GOLDILOCKS STACK

Digital leaders have struggled with stack and platform choices for the twenty-five years of the internet. They have bought their digital experience fully off the shelf from legacy platforms and found that, tens of millions of dollars later, their websites and apps don't look much different than Amazon's. They have tried to buy tools and hired armies of people to curate websites to optimize for their business—only to find that the scale and diversity of their seekers overwhelm them. They have tried to build robust digital organizations, setting up centers of excellence in Silicon Valley and aiming to turn into tech companies—only to find out that software development is a commitment to a long-term lifestyle, one that so many companies simply don't have. As they struggle with alternatives, digital leaders are confronted with the evolution from customer to seeker—while start-ups deeply understand the motivations of their customers and build novel, end-to-end experiences, raising the bar once again.

Technology has never been the only answer to these business challenges. But it is a big part of the solution. The DXP offers a new kind of promise—one that has prebuilt services so teams don't need the expertise or the gestation period to build the plumbing that all great digital properties need, accompanied by industry-leading AI to optimize for business goals and modern tools for business users to remain in control. It also offers built-in seeker centricity in a number of ways. With its API orientation, developers can innovate quickly and integrate multiple third-party services to serve the higher-order motivation of the seeker. With its AI capabilities, the platform will be able to process varied signals from the interactions of the human being that answer this question: "What should I show you next?"

The promise of the DXP is as much economic as technological. To use an analogy, we previously had a choice only between buying the cookie-cutter home and undertaking the lengthy project of building a custom home. Now we get to buy the frame of the house and put our own unique design elements into the interior, along with a beautiful paint job on the outside.

We get to market faster. We do it for less money. And with the built-in AI, our experiences just keep getting faster and better. That's the way to win.

The winner's technology stack harnesses the power of the three As and embeds it in a powerful, singular DXP that serves as the foundation of all digital experiences. On that platform, teams build highly innovative experiences that drive growth and iterate on their experience at hyperspeed. But building a winning digital experience does not end with the selection of the right technology stack. Winners must ensure that those experiences are built with the appropriate safeguards to protect against bad actors, unintended biases, and tolerance for inherent faults. That is the subject of our next chapter.

6

DESIGN FOR DISASTER

What does a digital disaster look like?

It can take many forms, and most digital team members can list them from their nightmares: a privacy breach, an unintended outcome of artificial intelligence (AI), a failure of service. Any one can take a formerly winning digital experience and send it right off the rails. The media are full of examples. The privacy breech at Equifax affected as much as half the U.S. population. An attack on Sony created an international incident when it angered North Korean dictator Kim Jong Un. And a hack of extramarital dating site Ashley Madison left millions of men with some serious explaining to do.

The stakes for companies and organizations have only gone up with the expansion of digital transformation. Online was once an option and then a channel, and now it's ingrained in all aspects of work. Sites simply can't go down. Customers' private information simply can't be mishandled. The results of a digital disaster can range anywhere from a fine to a death knell. Regulations are also getting involved in the journey—with the General Data Protection Regulation (GDPR), Europe's far-reaching privacy act, and its more recent California cousin, the California Consumer Privacy Act (CCPA), creating legal risks that result in other forms of disaster. No self-respecting digital team takes disaster lightly.

Table 6.1

The Core Tenets of a Digital Experience That Scales

Privacy	Privacy is about making sure that we honor the data property rights of our customers.
Security	Security is about the set of practices that ensure that our data and systems are protected from bad actors.
Reliability	Digital is not a division; it's the steel beams that hold the structure aloft. That's the good news. The reality that comes with it is that, quite simply, digital cannot go down. A winning digital experience must be fully reliable. Failure is not an option.
Performance	With the demands for instant gratification has come a wide array of tools like Kafka and Spark that enable real-time events: a click on a link, a change to a product name, or a new attribute of a product can be reflected immediately. Winning digital teams are increasingly designing experiences that deliver immediate joy.
Explainability	My lesson building a highly impactful AI-driven system has convinced me that for an AI-driven digital experience to work, trust is the key. Too many AI projects are thought of as offloads from human to machine when in fact a new workflow that intersperses human activity and AI inevitably needs to be designed to solve the problem at hand. To attack this problem, digital teams must do more than embrace AI. They must pull back the curtain and demystify AI. For too long, we allowed AI to operate in a black box. This has left too many unsure as to how the technology works and why it delivers as it does. A winning digital experience needs explainability.
Diversity	Unintended consequences are the next battlefield for AI and the potential disaster a winning digital team must confront. AI is everywhere and its consequences follow. For all the host of positive outcomes AI produces, the negative ones will grab the headlines: customer denied loans or credit cards, companies using hiring robots that engage in gender bias. One of the latest cases of problematic AI surrounds voice command assistants such as Siri and Alexa. Research suggests the technology understands men far more often than women and white speakers far more often than those of other races. Unintentional—but there it is.

For that reason, this chapter will be devoted to disasters—and how to stay ahead of them. I call the process design for disaster. It's the thinking that must go into the creation and permeate the management of a digital experience. Disasters can take many forms, but I've sorted them into three categories for this discussion: privacy and security, reliability and performance, and explainability and diversity.

PRIVACY AND SECURITY

Privacy and security are two sides of the same coin. Their unifying theme is safety. Privacy is about making sure that we honor the data property rights of our customers. After all, what they tell us about themselves doesn't belong to those of us who design and power the experience; it belongs to them. Security is about the set of practices that ensure our data and systems are protected from bad actors. To use an analogy, privacy is about defining the set of precious items I want to make sure don't get out—my email address, Social Security number, and bank account information. Security represents the locks we put on the drawers to protect that data but also the home alarm systems that we use to protect ourselves and the rest of our property and loved ones. They are related—but not the same.

Safety is at the core of digital trust. And trust is at the core of the customer's selection of their chosen service provider. Am I safe when I'm interacting with this site? Is this site safe when it's interacting with customers? Safety is the goal on either end of the digital transaction, and neither the customer nor the provider wants to be in danger. We want to be safe from those who would mine our data for their own purposes, and we want to be safe from bad actors who would steal our data and sell it to the highest bidder.

Privacy is a top concern for customers, and yet many know little about how to achieve it. Changing your password frequently can only get you so far. The onus is then on the digital team to design and manage the experience so as to safeguard the privacy of the user and the security of the site and its infrastructure.

I came to think about data privacy in my earliest days at Bloomreach. The world was already segmenting personally identifiable information (email addresses, payment data, etc.) from non–personally identifiable information (cookie IDs or user IDs that cannot be traced to individuals). The goal in the early days was simple: avoid designing a service that collected any kind of personally identifiable information for fear of needing to comply with a bunch of highly onerous regulations. If we could build a data-driven service at Bloomreach that crunched through a lot of data and added a lot of value but did not need personally identifiable information, that was the best case. That is how we started with our early search technologies. We knew only that user ID 1234 preferred blue blazers and products within a given price range. But we did not know their name, their billing information, or anything else about them. It turned out that just being able to know real-time preferences gave us some data, but increasingly the world of personalization needs to know more—including past transaction history, location, and other personally identifiable traits. The stakes had been raised, and the need for elevated privacy-protecting practices became foremost in my mind. The emergence of the GDPR in 2016 and its adoption in 2018 made this not just desirable but also required. I recall discussions with Tim Walters, a foremost digital experience and privacy expert. The threat of noncompliance with Europe's digital privacy laws was made real by the two tiers of administrative fines: 2–4 percent of global turnover depending on the tier. For most digital businesses, including some of the largest in the world—Google, Netflix, Amazon, and others—that's a lot of money! The GDPR woke us all up. Every conversation with a large client involved confirming GDPR compliance, all at a time when very few understood what it would take to comply. Years later, regulators in California would follow suit, adopting the CCPA and requiring businesses operating in the state to comply with privacy regulations, and several countries around the world would take similar steps.

So what have we learned about data privacy in the many years since the GDPR came out? Tim educated me that while the regulations may be long and complex, the prime directive is summarized in one of the early paragraphs of the law, which asserts that people should have control of their data. With that simple directive, the GDPR made personal data personal property, subject to all the same protections as other personal property. So what should we do as designers of personalized digital experiences if we want to use that personal property? First, we should ask customers if we can use it in the first place. Second, we should tell them what we plan to use it for and then not use it for anything beyond that or share it with anyone without their permission. Third, we should use only the minimum necessary. And finally, we should delete it when we are not using it.

Pretty straightforward, right? Hardly. Complying with the spirit of the GDPR requires a massive shift in terms of how we think about data. Most of Silicon Valley's tech companies were built on the fundamental principle that data is an asset, meant to be accumulated. The more data Google had about your search patterns, the less likely a competitor, even one with comparable software, could compete with it. The more data Facebook had about your likes, dislikes, friends, and interests, the less likely a competing social network could compete with it. "Data is the new oil" was the refrain we heard from several magazines and newspapers. Many digital leaders would view the regulations as roadblocks on their way to accumulating the most valuable asset of the digital economy. That is a point of view that is not only counter to the regulatory regime but also counter to the wishes of our customers. Equally, regulators ignore the practicalities of providing a high degree of fine-grained control of data elements in a world where data collection is built into thousands of systems and data is stored in hundreds of databases and consumed by hundreds of applications. Even if I wanted to delete your data, how practical would it be to find it? And by the way, how do we reconcile the growing fears and regulations around digital privacy with the very real surveys that suggest that an overwhelming number of millennials value the functionality and convenience of an app over its security and privacy?

The answer lies in focusing on our use of data over and above its collection. Instead of an arms race to collect data, we need an arms race to create highly beneficial services that use data to assure maximum benefit to our customer.

To deliver privacy, customers will need digital teams to be more transparent about what is happening behind the scenes of any digital experience. They'll need digital teams to be truthful about what has *already* happened to their data. The truth is that we are throwing off so much data—all day, every day—that keeping it all private is a lost cause. That ship has sailed. Our data is out and is being collected en masse. I don't mean our Social Security numbers and medical test results. I'm talking about the data generated by the apps we use. Apps are spewing data about where we go, what we eat, what we buy, who we admire, and how we communicate. All this is collected in massive amounts every day. If we engage with an app when we're using Wi-Fi, we generate data, and that is collected, stored, sorted, and scanned by companies and governments. It's in use right now. Shutting the door—in such a way that our data stays entirely behind our own walls—is unlikely to happen. Certainly digital teams should comply with the GDPR and other privacy regulations by collecting as little data as possible and enabling customers to control it. But most customers will gladly trade some access to their data in return for a highly valuable service that makes use of it.

That data is generated and collected is a given. What happens next is a topic for debate—one that digital teams must address. What's happening to that data? Is it being used for the customer's benefit? Is it managed with the customer in mind and in ways the customer will like? This is really what customers mean when they talk about privacy. I am perfectly comfortable with Apple collecting my mapping and navigation data if it uses the information to give me a better commuting experience. That dovetails with the reason I use the navigation app in the first place, so I have no quarrel with my whereabouts being noted and collected by Apple. That's a modicum of privacy I give up with a clear benefit to me in return.

Now what if my data is being collected and I'm not the beneficiary? Let's look at Facebook. Facebook collects data from my posts and from my friends list and provides it to advertisers who target me with marketing campaigns. Now I'm unhappy about the state of my privacy because the loss of it resulted in a benefit to someone else, not me. I signed up for Facebook so I could communicate with my friends and family. No one uses Facebook because they want to be targeted by advertisers. When that happens, it's clear to me that my privacy has been leveraged for someone else's financial gain. I'm annoyed that I've lost my privacy and someone else is the beneficiary.

This is the dynamic that digital teams must address. It's not whether or not sites or apps are collecting data. They are. The issue is how that data is being used and how digital teams are communicating that use to customers. Indeed, the most important thing the members of a digital team can take away from the privacy conversation is that they must ensure that the data they collect is put to use to benefit the customer *today*. The idea of building a stockpile of data to either benefit my advertisers or use for some future innovation violates both the privacy regulations and the trust contract we make with our customers.

A sensible data-use strategy should then be accompanied by transparency. Without transparency, customers are left to wonder what you're doing with their data. That does not breed the kind of trust that's necessary for a lifetime customer.

Transparency needs a transformation, says Tim. What companies and organizations are doing now isn't serving anyone. Take a routine privacy tactic—the cookie consent form. It pops up almost immediately when you arrive at a website, and, says Tim, it's everything that is wrong with the privacy conversation today. "The problem is that the cookie consent form was generated by the compliance department." Because it was designed by lawyers, it protects the company from legal action but does nothing at all to serve the customer or the brand. "You're not doing anything that's going to get you in trouble, but you're actively undermining the customer experience. These notices are, almost without exception, totally unbranded. Separate from the brand story, separate from whatever the site's goal may be. You're lucky if it's got the company logo on it."

The cookie consent form may satisfy the requirement of the GDPR or CCPA. But it doesn't help your digital experience, and it does nothing to reassure the customer that the site is concerned with the state of their privacy. Why do you want that information? What are you going to use it for? Will it benefit me, or are you going to follow Facebook and sell it to someone so they can target me with ads I don't want? The cookie consent form answers none of those questions. For the customer who clicks "OK" just to move on with the digital experience, a veil of mistrust has already fallen over the relationship—in just the first few seconds of engagement.

The fix, says Tim, is to wrest the privacy issue from the legal department and give it to the digital team to address—not from a compliance perspective but from a customer happiness perspective. Tell customers what they want to know about data collection and usage. For example, suppose the consent form didn't pop up at the start of a visit but instead appeared when the site had a reason to collect data. Say you're shopping and you put something in your virtual cart. A pop-up could appear with this offer: "Could we place a cookie on your browser that will maintain your shopping cart and allow you to return to it at a later date?" Now, instead of a blanket request, you've made what Tim calls a just-in-time request. You want data; the customer wants the convenience of a virtually maintained shopping cart. Now your customer not only says yes but also has evidence that you care about their privacy. After all, you asked nicely for the data rather than just grabbing it.

Some companies are already following the just-in-time data request process. Tim points to IKEA, which generated buzz in the privacy community with an eight-minute YouTube video posted by the company's chief information officer. It explains that data collection is a process that requires a trigger—a reason that could be conveyed to the customer.

When you explain the benefit, customers are more likely to say yes. They know what data you want and how it will benefit them—not some third party.

This is a conversation most companies are not yet having with their customers. But it's a level of transparency that would build trust.

We want data to innovate and elevate the digital experience. To get it, digital teams need to broach this subject with customers rather than simply bullying them into signing away their data at the start of the visit.

Flip the coin to security, and trust takes on even greater weight. Now both the customer and the digital experience are united in their quest to be safe. The customer may have willingly handed over their data to the digital experience, but they want to know it's not going to be hijacked by Russian pirates. Digital teams have a similar nightmare around outside bad actors wreaking havoc.

To achieve safety for all, security must be part of the digital team.

This sounds obvious, but it wasn't always standard operating procedure. Ross Williams, Bloomreach's former head of information security, remembers when that wasn't so. He began his cybersecurity career in the U.S. Marines and then moved to the business world. For a long time, he says, cybersecurity was considered a subset of IT rather than its own entity. This made it hard for security experts to be heard. "Security tried to influence business using fear and cried wolf too much. At some point, business quit listening."

As privacy and security issues proliferated, security and business had to find a way to come together. That began to happen as security emerged as its own presence at the table—an executive presence. Now boards have recognized the reputational and legal issues at stake, Ross says, raising the profile of security within digital teams. That said, much of security has to be defensive. "I don't think hacks are avoidable. At the end of the day, there's always going to be a door left open. Businesses have to assume a certain amount of risk to operate," says Ross. "What's imperative is that a company puts in place the means and mechanisms to minimize the impact when that does happen." Ross is a member of Bloomreach's global operations team. He has a broad purview—across legal, IT, engineering, HR, facilities, and marketing. Our security team touches every part of an organization. That is how it should be in digital. Security needs to be built into the fabric of a digital organization. I see too many of our digital customers where that is not the case. The "infosec" function sits in or alongside legal or IT. It is viewed in the same way as legal—a cost of doing business. The result is that business practitioners are rarely familiar with security best practices, software is rarely built securely, and marketing data is often not housed securely. Like any major initiative, our data security team has a road map. That road map is never done, but every quarter we make progress. In some quarters, it may come with increased security across our physical locations. In other quarters, we may be enabling virtual private clouds in our infrastructure.

The worlds of systems, data security, and data privacy have been significantly impacted by the three As we discussed earlier in this book. Indeed, we now live in a world where the digital experience is not just built with internal data by internal software. We use third-party (often open source) software, ingest data from external ambient sources, and call services provided by external application programming interfaces (APIs). Indeed, data may not be the new oil, but it is certainly the new water. It flows everywhere and comes from everywhere. All these practices massively multiply risk. Much as we place guards on our national borders, we need to shift our security thinking to the points of ingress and egress in our data and systems infrastructure. The key is to be highly intentional: to collect only the required data, to tag it so that it can be identified later, to keep it offline until it needs to be brought online, and, when it is online, to limit access in a highly auditable manner. Just as any good security system will have multiple points of redundancy, so, too, must our security infrastructure.

RELIABILITY AND PERFORMANCE

In the early days of e-commerce, a digital experience was an option. Now it's a requirement. While companies and organizations first looked at their digital experiences as an add-on, now many rely on them to deliver the core elements of their products and services. Digital is not a division; it's the steel beams that hold the structure aloft. That's the good news. The reality that comes with it is that, quite simply, digital cannot go down. A winning digital experience must be fully reliable. Failure is not an option.

This is no small challenge, since failure is a real and constant danger. The more technologically advanced we've become, the more opportunity there is for an unfortunate accident . . . or mistake . . . or unintended outcome. As we have added complexity to our digital experiences, we have added opportunity for things to go wrong.

Xun Wang, Bloomreach's chief technology officer, knows that whatever technology may trumpet as its latest accomplishment, the challenge comes from what lies beneath. "In today's world, you don't need to go out and build a computer processor; somebody else did that. You don't need to develop RAM; somebody did that. The fact of the matter is today's technology is built on top of the last fifty years of technology. Because of the complexity of the stack, you cannot guarantee that everything underneath is going to be 100 percent." Resilience must be built into the applications to ensure their reliability.

The power of designing resilient and high-performance systems is no easy task. In many ways, the emergence of public cloud infrastructure has solved a lot of problems. Specifically, public clouds started by designing for hardware failures; storage, network, and computing failures could be mitigated with virtual machines, unlimited storage clusters, and redundant nodes. But much as the large banks have at times been "too big to fail," public cloud infrastructure—specifically, Amazon Web Services (AWS)—runs a lot of the internet and is starting to present a similar risk. While Amazon certainly does a good job, we discovered the importance of mitigating that risk a couple of years ago when AWS went down and some of the largest websites and apps on the internet went down with it.

Although we run much of our infrastructure on AWS, Bloomreach hummed along uninterrupted. That is because on top of AWS, Bloomreach engineers built a layer of resilience to route around a failed availability zone to a functional one. The software that redirected web traffic was not native to AWS; it was an extra layer of resilience built proactively to protect against corner cases. And it sure came in handy. Indeed, many of Bloomreach's largest clients are on or are moving their digital infrastructure to the public cloud. It's a wise decision. It's highly unlikely that the investment a digital brand can make can ever replicate the infrastructure performance and resilience of a big public cloud. But as in the case of AWS's availability zone failure, it is not a replacement for designing an application that is built on the assumption of infrastructure failure rather than always counting on a 100 percent uptime system. Relying on a public cloud also enables an organization to rely on a long list of innovations that drive improving resilience. For example, EKS, Amazon's Elastic Kubernetes Service, allows Kubernetes to be available from the cloud—one more thing that a digital experience builder doesn't have to worry about as they think about the necessary infrastructure for their application.

At Bloomreach, we certainly haven't always been perfect despite our early adoption of public clouds. The most significant outage in Bloomreach's history was not the result of machines going awry. As with so many failures, it was caused by human error. Specifically, we were updating a pretty innocuous configuration management file, which drives customer-specific configurations in Bloomreach's large cluster of digital properties. The configuration change was not a software release and therefore did not go through the level of rigorous testing that a typical release would. It turned out, however, that an error in the inputs in that file caused pernicious downstream effects, and a whole cascading set of systems gradually went down. Debugging the problem was particularly challenging because as each system went down, it appeared that the underlying software for that system was operating satisfactorily. Monitoring did not catch the system because it was built to consider system uptime, not inappropriate data. The number of components in the system, all highly interdependent, presented challenging real-time pressures for the engineers who were on the case. All the while, our customers were starting to scream!

Ultimately the problem was found, but just as the problem cascaded through our system, restoring it required cascading a fix.

All told, the cascading failure reminded us that our systems are only as good as their weakest link—especially when you have the incredibly unstable element of human input to consider. One changed input by a human user can create a cascading failure, in which the changed element undermines the functionality of a connected element and nodes begin to topple like dominoes. As Xun muses, "You never imagine that a small, innocuous change could take it all down, but it happens." Since our experience with this, Bloomreach has put in place a rigorous change management process and associated monitoring of data outputs. The problem should never resurface. But it does teach us the very serious lesson that as our systems become larger and more complex, with more components and external dependencies, our vulnerability increases. Going back to our border example, just as we want guards on the border, we want multiple points of egress and ingress, just in case one of the primary arteries is blocked, and a careful process for letting the right people in and out.

At its core, a winning digital team is charged with building a resilient and high-performing application. And no amount of reliance on cloud infrastructure can take away from the criticality of that task. At Bloomreach, our search and content management applications simply can't go down. The teams charged with every major component are responsible for designing highly fault-tolerant systems.

Building something that doesn't go down doesn't always mean it's going to be superfast. In today's digital experiences, the consumer's patience when waiting for the page or app to load is incredibly low, raising the bar for what we all build and all of the subcomponents it's built on. For example, Bloomreach search is built on the open-source Solr stack. As we discover use cases for complex search needs, we test not only the boundaries of our own technology but also those of our open-source stacks. Ensuring that we can deliver a high-performance system requires us to have deep expertise not just in the systems we build but also in the underlying Solr technology.

Low-latency digital experiences are increasingly built on real-time systems. No longer are Bloomreach's e-commerce customers willing to wait hours for a change in the price of a product to manifest in their tools or on their site. They expect updates to be instantaneous. With the demands for instant gratification has come a wide array of tools like Kafka and Spark that enable real-time events: a click on a link, a change to a product name, or the addition of a new attribute of a product can be reflected immediately. Winning digital teams are increasingly designing experiences that deliver immediate joy.

Building high-performing and resilient systems starts with the design of the teams themselves. In the last several years, we have seen a hotly contested debate between advocates of "devops" and advocates of "prodops." In essence, the question becomes, Who is responsible for the operations of a digital experience? In a devops model, each development cell takes responsibility for its own operational resilience. In a prodops model, a centralized operations team works across the development teams. In the early days of most development teams, including those at Bloomreach, the devops model typically wins out. Why rely on an external team to push software into production? Great digital teams want to control their own success. As teams, components, and system complexity grow, the argument tips in favor of prodops. A centralized team can look across risks of cascading failures, component dependencies, security requirements, infrastructure budgets, and release processes to add a gate to the innovation process. Prodops teams now serve the very important function of ensuring the whole system operates to further the organization's goals. Certainly velocity can be a casualty of such an approach. In my experience, the more mission critical the digital experience application is, the more often the prodops approach wins out. The less mission critical the application is, the more often the devops model is the right one.

EXPLAINABILITY AND DIVERSITY

Finally, designing for disaster means facing the realities of unintended consequences. AI has a dark side, and it starts with the fact that AI is fundamentally opaque. Whether it is a personalization system recommending a movie to you or a self-driving car navigating the road or a diagnosis in an MRI, often AI is in charge. Usually the motivation of the AI system is pure: to sift through the reams of data and find a great movie, get you safely to your destination, or accurately diagnose your health challenge. Unfortunately the reality can at times diverge from the motivation.

I discovered this firsthand through my experience at Bloomreach. In the early days of the company's history, I pulled together a team of data scientists and engineers who were involved in designing AI and machine learning–based systems at Google and Facebook. We sought to solve "the relevance problem on the Web." Specifically, we wanted to figure out how to design a system that would predict the most relevant piece of content or product to show someone that would maximize the revenue of the brand publishing the website or app. Like any good AI system, it would start with quality data. Ideally we would approach our enterprise customers and ask them to provide a well-formed consumer profile— one that included all past purchases, interactions, rejections, and preferences. They would also give us a full catalog of products and content. We would feed that into our AI system and start optimizing what to show to whom. Unfortunately, no one seemed to have that data readily available. So we didn't let perfect be the enemy of good and built a system of collectors that could ingest real-time interactions on the website and a basic feed of products and could start to drive the algorithms. Herein lies an important practical challenge of designing for AI: it's important to assume that you *won't* have the highest-quality data and to build a system that can add value despite that.

Once we assembled the data, we started to build our algorithms and optimized revenue per visit, propensity to buy at the user level, relevance of search results, and more and more. The early versions of Bloomreach's search and AI technology were a bit of a black box. You fed it data and specified what outcome you were looking to achieve.

It spit back the perfect set of products or content to achieve that goal. Unfortunately our first version didn't sell. Our customers subjected us to highly onerous A/B tests. We needed to bring in experts to explain why the AI was making the decisions it was. When there was a problem, we had a very hard time disentangling what was due to poor-quality data inputs and what might have been a weakness in the algorithm. Even when we overcame those obstacles, the people we were working with were fundamentally skeptical. Often we were replacing tasks that would otherwise be done by a human being. And those human beings subjected the machine to a much higher standard than they used for other human beings.

Ultimately, we embarked on a multiyear project to turn our AI-based optimization system from a black box system to a white box system. We built diagnostics so that people could understand why the AI was making the decision it was. We built monitoring systems so that administrators could understand how and what data was flowing into the system. We went further and started to give a high degree of control over the end-user experience to marketers and merchandisers so that they could override the machine. In essence, we evolved the system from pure machine to human plus machine. No doubt the machine was still doing the heavy lifting, so we were still offloading repetitive manual tasks. But human beings were fully in charge. The success of our product skyrocketed after we took those steps. Now, instead of being skeptical of the machine, marketers and merchandisers could defend the decisions and actions of the AI. Building a system that enables humans and machines to work cooperatively was nontrivial. We needed to make sure human beings would be in charge but also wouldn't inadvertently make changes that negatively impacted business outcomes. We also discovered that in addition to governing the system, human beings would always have business context that the machine simply didn't have. They may know that a given dress is trending at the moment or that the chief financial officer has started to care a lot more about margin than growth or that millennials are a new and important target market. Ultimately, the machine would learn those things, but human beings knew them intuitively through their work.

My lesson building a highly impactful AI-driven system has convinced me that for an AI-driven digital experience to work, trust is the key. Too many AI projects are thought of as offloads from human to machine when in fact a new workflow that intersperses human activity and AI inevitably needs to be designed to solve the problem at hand. To attack this problem, digital teams must do more than embrace AI. They must pull back the curtain and demystify AI. For too long we allowed AI to operate in a black box. This has left too many unsure as to how the technology works and why it delivers as it does.

A winning digital experience needs explainability.

Explainability is a relatively new concept. It's the idea that AI is not magic but rather a series of decisions and consequence that can—and must—be explained. Will Uppington, who as Chief Product Officer for Bloomreach from the start of the company, was a key driver of the algorithm and AI technology we built, and who now runs his own company devoted to explainability, Truera, says "When people first experience AI, they say 'Wow, this is amazing. It's kind of like magic.' They initially accept the idea that smart people know what they don't know and it's going to create some magic algorithm that gets everything right." But those expectations are impossible to meet for an imperfect technology and when things go wrong, trust crumbles and now AI is to blame. The answer, he says, is not just in the technology to explain AI but also in the company leadership. "The technology to explain AI now exists and needs to be embraced. AI can be understood even by non-data scientists. Now, we need to push the organization to prioritize understanding it and to create mutual understanding between the business and technical teams. That's how you build trust." The area of AI explainability only becomes more important as we move in the direction of deep learning, where AI is making ever more complex and nuanced decisions. It also becomes important in categories of AI-driven decisions that are highly consequential. It is one thing for Netflix to recommend a bad movie. On the other hand, the legal and human implications of a misdiagnosis or a miscalculated credit score can be much more dire. We need humans in the loop to stand up for AI.

One of the primary blind spots that has emerged in AI centers on diversity and inclusion. When institutions deploy AI to make decisions, they may well feel as if the use of technology is more "fair." By taking humans out of the equation, they've removed potential bias. But in fact, bias can live in AI, even if that wasn't its intended design. It's not hard to see. Say I need a software engineer. If I power up LinkedIn and begin searching, chances are good my results will be men who are graduates of schools I attended and who match my ethnic background. I didn't ask for that filter, but the AI behind the search function is trying to divine my preferences based on my behavior and data points. It wasn't designed to address an inclusion question or solve a diversity issue—so it doesn't. I may feel as though I am conducting an unbiased search by using technology. But in truth, the technology is executing bias on my behalf.

Unintended consequences are the next battlefield for AI and the potential disaster a winning digital team must confront. AI is everywhere and its consequences follow. For all the host of positive outcomes AI produces, the negative ones will grab the headlines: customers denied loans or credit cards, companies using hiring robots that engage in gender bias. One of the latest cases of problematic AI surrounds voice command assistants such as Siri and Alexa. Research suggests the technology understands men far more often than women and white speakers far more often than those of other races. Unintentional—but there it is.

A winning digital team will fully embrace all the modern technology trends that will shape highly differentiated experiences. They will work to pull data in from ambient sources. They will modularize system development and gain extraordinary leverage from the API economy. They will leverage AI to solve challenging data-intensive problems. But they will also know that none of these technologies is or will be perfect. They will plan on systems crashing, requests to servers timing out, bad actors using these new entry points to attack them, regulations promoting ever more taxing privacy protections, and AI-based decisions being both imperfect and untrustworthy. Winning digital teams know the future looks bright but is not insulated from lightning strikes. To put it directly, they will design for disaster.

A business needs innovation and proactive design, business intuition and technical expertise. Winning comes down to building the right digital team.

7

RECAST YOUR TEAM TO SHIP

John Koryl and I have worked together three times over ten years: at Williams-Sonoma, Neiman Marcus, and Canadian Tire. Each time I've watched him work his magic, driving growth, innovation, and transformation. John has a detailed playbook for driving digital success.

At the heart of his playbook is the ability to use data both in decision-making and in real time to power digital experiences. Ten years later I've realized that winning digital teams, like those led by John, have data in their DNA, and the trends we have seen around AI and data have transformed every role on the digital team.

But data DNA is not the only shift we are seeing across digital roles. Winning digital teams view the experience as a product. What does that mean? Many companies have products. Telecommunications businesses view their wireless plans as products. Scientific manufacturers view the lab equipment they make as products. Software businesses view their software as products. But when I talk about experience as a product, *I am talking about the way the seeker experiences the product digitally.* Both T-Mobile and Verizon sell wireless services, but how I find, buy, and engage with their products is the core of the digital experience. Many companies will think of that as "just marketing." But winners know better. They know that the best companies integrate their offering with the way their customers access that offering digitally. Can they estimate their usage digitally? Can they provision the phone without speaking to someone? Can they bill other purchases through their mobile plan? The seeker will tell them what to build, but if the team members don't view the digital experience as a product, they will kick all those requests over to marketing and hope for the best. And a digitally native brand will destroy them. If, on the other hand, they treat the digital experience as a product, they will ship new versions of the experience frequently, iterating to business success. The digital team must be product oriented, just as its Silicon Valley counterparts will be, to win big.

Finally, as John told me, "Digital is a row, not a column."

What does that mean? It's actually a blueprint for the creation of a winning digital team. It means that looking at digital purely through the lens of e-commerce is a huge mistake. The digital experience goes much beyond e-commerce. It impacts the supply chain. It impacts how store associates communicate with their customers. It impacts how business-to-business (B2B) companies empower their sellers. Digital is at the heart of everything—which means it needs to be present everywhere. So many businesses will hire a chief digital officer (CDO) and give them the resources to bring on a digital team—maybe one that is empowered to own the P&L for e-commerce. That's a good first step. But if digital is the heartbeat of the company, that CDO needs to be able to place reports in every major function of the company and influence all the surrounding operational processes. World-class digital teams include a direct team that represents the P&L of the "digital-only" business—online travel or e-commerce or online media. But they also have digital ambassadors who reside across marketing, sales, merchandising, technology, and a wide range of other functions.

In this chapter, I'll take you on a tour of the digital dream team. Depending on the size of your organization, not every role needs to be filled by an individual person. Some teams will just have two or three people. Some will have two or three thousand. But all winning digital teams will span a set of six key competencies, and we'll

Figure 7.1 The digital dream team draws from every corner of the company.

review them here, along with examples of winners who have held these roles. Your product designers will deeply understand seeker intent and help visualize a future alternative. Your product manager will define exactly what that experience needs to be. Your technology team will build it. Your site merchandising team will bring it to life on your digital experience, and your marketing team will bring the droves of digital seekers in the door. Your CDO will lead the way.

CHIEF DIGITAL OFFICER

The CDO has many names. In certain businesses, the leader of the digital business is a chief technology officer (CTO). Often they will be the chief marketing officer (CMO). Sometimes they might be a president of e-commerce. Occasionally, they will be the chief information officer (CIO). Whatever the title, the job is the same: take us to the digital promised land. CDOs were born out of the fact that most businesses don't start digital. At some point, the noise around digital causes the board and the CEO to say "We need digital DNA in the company." They look for strong individuals out of technology companies and bring them on as CDOs. Not every business needs their digital leader to be a CDO—they can have one of the many titles described above. But every business needs the role. Without the right leadership profile, losing is predestined.

A great CDO is a technology-oriented business leader or a business-oriented technology leader. They are true unicorns. John Strain is one such unicorn. He grew up in the early days of digital at Andersen Consulting and Fort Point Capital Partners, where he built and delivered websites and e-commerce stores in the early days of the internet. He spent three years as vice president of IT at Gap, Inc., and eleven years at Williams-Sonoma; then he became chief digital and technology officer at Gap, Inc., where he leads the full digital team. John basically grew up in IT but had enough business experience and savvy to ultimately be in a position to connect the dots. He talks about the need to dive into deep analytics technology, ensure the site stays up over holidays, understand marketing attribution, guide search optimization, and understand customer acquisition. He is a true hybrid—equally comfortable with the *Wall Street Journal* and *Hacker News*.

But not all CDOs start their career in technology. Christina Callas is a world-class CDO, leading the digital teams at Total Wine & More. Her degree is in economics, and she earned an MBA from Columbia Business School. She describes her first job in digital as approaching the leadership at Aeropostale and asking them "What project is not getting enough attention?" in the early days of the Web. The company assigned her to e-commerce. After three years at Aeropostale, she joined Hudson's Bay Company—whose department stores included Lord & Taylor and Hudson's Bay. During that formative career experience, she relaunched all the web properties, developed digital marketing programs, and orchestrated a multichannel transformation of the business. Along the way, she came to be well versed in technology—keenly understanding the key e-commerce systems and how they work. When I met her at Hudson's Bay, and later at Total Wine, she completely understood how data science and algorithms could positively impact the wine experience. She is yet another digital unicorn, equally facile in the worlds of business and technology.

Why does the duality matter so much? Because great digital leaders must connect the dots between the key technology choices or investments and the financial impacts of those choices. Unlike those many other roles, CDOs don't get to simply outsource those choices to a CTO or a CIO. They might partner with one of those individuals, but they are on the line for results—and technology is the lifeblood of any digital business. Equally, so many great technologists can't prioritize what will move the needle. Technology choices abound. The hard part is figuring out which of the many initiatives not to take on. That requires keen business insight.

When I asked John Strain what the attributes of a great CDO are, he described the CDO role as "A little bit creative. A little bit engineer. A little bit showman." We get the engineer and the creative parts, but why do we need a showman as a CDO?

Because a key responsibility of the CDO is to be the Sherpa who inspires and teaches the rest of the organization what excellence in digital looks like. John does this by organizing leadership sessions and bringing in experts from partners like Facebook to talk about the future of social media or Google to talk about the future of search. Education and inspiration are a core part of what makes the CDO job impactful.

The teaching isn't just for the team. It is often for the CEO and the board. Christina told me the story of a consulting engagement she did in a prior role where she was advising the CEO on digital. When she told the CEO "My job is to demystify digital for you," she watched a wave of relief come over his face. I've presented at numerous board meetings of Bloomreach clients, mostly at the request of the CDO, to share our data and thinking and to help educate the board on what it takes to win in digital. Great CEOs are wise enough to understand their blind spots and welcome a partner who can help show the way. So many CEOs of successful companies didn't get there because of digital. But to stay there, they need digital to work.

Successful CDOs understand that their relationship with the CEO is key. Digital takes money and sponsorship. It involves breaking some glass. Christina shares with me that using Bloomreach algorithms to drive the wine assortment is not a no-brainer at Total Wine.

Change takes sponsorship. The most successful businesses do not leave the CDO alone to fight the battles. The whole team gets behind digital. I spoke to Christina about the companies she considered before she joined Total Wine, and she shared the story of the company she turned down—a lucrative opportunity with all the empowerment in the world. The company was recruiting three C-level executives, a CDO and two others. The two other candidates had no digital in their background. Christina turned the job down. Digital is a C-level team sport. Nowadays, she says, "everyone knows enough about digital to drive me a little bit crazy." It sounds like she prefers that to being left alone to steer the ship. John Koryl offers similar advice to CEOs: "Give everyone the ability to vote me off the island." If all the other C-level executives are not enrolled in the choice of CDO, the CDO is likely to fail.

Great CDOs have a playbook for repeated success. It's not that different from the strategies of so many C-level roles in that it starts by winning big and winning early. John Koryl starts every new role with an intense focus on digital marketing. Why? Because marketing, unlike technology, does not require you to rebuild anything. It is all about optimizing spend to acquire the most profitable customers at the lowest cost. In an existing digital business, it's the fastest, least disruptive way to impact. He follows that up by focusing on the base experiences: making digital shopping and interactions easy and frictionless. Finally he identifies what makes the business special and brings it to life digitally. Typically executed in exactly that order, the playbook works. While phrased differently, Christina has her own playbook. She is centered on making digital shopping easy on totalwine.com—making the basics great. She intends to follow that up by building the magical experience people have walking into a Total Wine store, where a guide helps them find the perfect bottle of wine. She intends to bring joy to the digital experience, the kind that comes from discovering and sharing an incredible bottle of red.

One day CEOs of most businesses will be digital natives. When that day comes, we won't need CDOs. Until then, the hunt for unicorns is on.

But great CDOs know that they are only as good as their teams—talent is the currency for winning. Let's meet the rest of the dream team.

DESIGN

For so many years, design has been an afterthought. In so many technology businesses, key product decisions were made by product managers and engineers, with strong influence from sales and marketing. Design? That was for the creative types who would come in at the end and make it pretty. But Apple and, more recently, Pinterest have taught the rest of us that users value great design. They may never tell you that your design is the reason they didn't adopt or buy your product, but they will show it in the lack of affection they have for your product. Or conversely, when users fall in love with a product, great design is almost always why.

For this reason, product designers need to be a part of the dream team. You start by ensuring they have a first-class role in the pod—right there with your product managers and your technology team. A great product designer will always start with the "why" question. Albert Wang joined Bloomreach after spending a number of years designing key parts of the user experience at LinkedIn. He is a well-rounded product leader, but his heart has always been in design. I asked him what makes great product design, and he told me a story that he heard from an early professor about the design of the MP3 player. The story is all about abstracting away from the features of the MP3 player and asking the key question: Why do people buy portable music carriers? It turns out that they highly value personalizing a playlist and having a nearly limitless number of songs on the playlist—all at high fidelity and all mobile. Of course, asking this key question would ultimately enable Apple to transform hardware in the music industry—with the iPod, the iPod Mini, and ultimately the iPhone, with integrated music-playing capabilities. But the story doesn't stop there. Abstracting the problem enabled Apple to think beyond the device to the overall system—ultimately including the earphones, iTunes, iTunes radio, billing, and software. The ability to buy a song for $1 was equally as instrumental in upending the music industry as the original iPod. Apple has always embraced abstractions and delivered systems that are incredibly difficult to compete with.

Sound familiar? It should—because *abstracting* is another way of saying "find your seeker." Sure, we should expect product designers to have a strong creative eye to help visualize a winning digital experience, but they play a key role in discovering what that experience should be. A great product designer is key to the kind of user research that helps create disruptive experiences. User research has certainly changed in the last several years. At the core of it, designers have always embraced *shadowing*, the practice of observing how a user completes a task, where the pains and the opportunities are. Shadowing can be much more effective than surveying or interviewing because it tells us what the user or the customer actually does rather than what they tell us they do. But you can't exactly shadow someone at three a.m. when they get up in the middle of the night to do something. Enter data. The emergence of data as one of the key themes of digital experiences has required product designers to get a lot more analytical. The data tells us where users are getting stuck and where they are getting frustrated.

Increasingly, product designers don't come from where we expect them to—that is, from creative backgrounds. A very large percentage of product designers comes with a computer science background. They clearly have decided that it can be a lot more fun to engage in abstractions and design experiences that directly touch human beings than to write back-end code. They also have the skills to run design workshops and design sprints, as we do so often with our customers.

The product designer on your team is ultimately responsible for three critical functions. First, they work with user researchers or conduct the research themselves to uncover the hidden seeker. Second, they bring a vision of the offering or solution to life in the form of a prototype or a mock—enabling you to validate or invalidate that solution before making the much more expensive investments in technology development or sales and marketing. Third, they apply their creative expertise to bring beautiful design to life. Previous incarnations of digital teams limited the product designer to the final activity, which meant they were a shared service, like finance or HR, rather than a core part of the digital experience team.

That's a mistake. Every digital experience journey starts with great design thinking.

PRODUCT

What exactly is product? Doesn't nearly every business have a product—and therefore a product manager? Staffing this role requires an understanding of the way the word is used in Silicon Valley. Product, in the world at large, is a thing—in many cases, an object. It's the good or service that comes off the production line. That's what we've been trained to call a product.

In Silicon Valley, the word—and the job—takes a much wider view. *Product* in a digital context means the digital product—that is, the digital experience. It's not a title that refers to what my company makes. It's a job committed to the experience of my digital consumer. The experience is the product, not the good or service we may sell. Think of it in this context: the developers on the digital team will be the ones building the digital experience. It's the product manager who tells them what to build. So many organizations have been making a transition from digital project managers to product managers. While digital project managers are totally focused on execution, product managers concentrate on defining what makes sense to execute on. Legacy organizations have IT teams that undertake projects and project managers that support them. Modern digital organizations have development teams that build the experience and product managers that define them.

Product managers in the technology industry have often been described as CEOs-in-training. Indeed, great product managers certainly need to have multiple skills. They need to have some technical knowledge to work with the engineering team. They need to have an understanding of your distribution strategy, ideally building capabilities into the product that aid that distribution. They need to have a view of the customer and the industry. They need to be great communicators. They need to balance strategy with execution. They take all the arrows when it doesn't work and can receive all the accolades when it does. Whoa! Tough job.

But a great digital product manager has one core responsibility: to define and build the road map for the digital experience in a way that uniquely captures the heart and mind of the seeker. I met one such product leader a few years ago when Brooke Logan, of HD Supply, one of the largest industrial distributors in North America, spoke at Bloomreach's customer event. Brooke grew up at Lowe's, one of the leading home improvement properties on the Web. She discovered product early in her career and, over the time she spent at Lowe's, owned many facets of the digital experience. She is right to believe that a level of connection to the customer is critical to her success: What does that individual think and need and feel? Brooke says she elevated her execution when she was working at Lowe's as a product manager and undertook a renovation of her own home. Living the customer experience made her a better and more empathetic product manager.

"You need to know the customer use cases, of course, backwards and forwards. But then you need to live that customer experience. You need to *be* them. That's how you get good at this role," she says. Every time she would go home to renovate, she would figure out her frustrations and come to work intent on fixing the digital experience for home improvement. Brooke today owns multiple parts of the digital experience at HD Supply—including find, checkout, and the other aspects of what we experience on the website. That kind of specific ownership is critical; it enables her to get up every day and work with her team to optimize a segment of the digital experience rather than being defocused with all the many tasks that come her way.

Product is the ultimate high-distraction job. Everyone—the boss, the boss's boss, and everyone on the team—has an opinion about what the digital product should be. A key attribute of a successful product manager is the ability to listen intently and adapt often but stay grounded by a core point of view on the direction of the product. At Bloomreach, we call this the product point of view. Peter Thiel, in his book *Zero to One*, describes it as "the secret." It is the raison d'etre for the product. It is the unique insight, derived from the seeker, that desperately calls for the product to exist, and therefore it must be a core influencer of the road map. If the product manager goes too far in the point-of-view direction, the product can become disconnected from reality. If the product manager builds only what the customer or user tells them to build, the product will lose its soul. Brooke talks of the sales team that was advocating for a feature on the website, one that was lightly used by the customers. She needed to get to the heart of the "why" and argued that just because Amazon has it doesn't mean HD Supply needs to have it. The market will always pull the product to fill gaps offered by competitors. It is the job of the product manager to often say no and stick to the point of view.

In fact, Brooke's proudest career accomplishment was redesigning Lowe's product detail page and winning awards for it. But it wasn't that she added a whole bunch of capabilities to the experience. In fact, she removed a whole bunch of features that simply weren't being used and that cluttered the experience. That takes battling. No doubt, someone in the company loved each of those features— otherwise, they would not have been built. Great product managers let the past go and obsess over what the customer is saying now.

Product managers sit at the nexus of the interdisciplinary team and must be evangelists of and for the digital offering—always communicating value and execution timelines with everyone.

Once a hypothesis is formed and validated, it is the product manager's job to design the road map. That's a big job. Typically there will be four to eight developers for every product manager, meaning that whatever the product manager decides, you will be investing four to eight times as much building it. Every winning digital team can trace its roots to great product management.

DEVELOPER

There's a joke in the tech world that goes like this:

Where's the hardest place to hire a great software developer?
Silicon Valley.
Where's the next hardest?
Everywhere else.

Developers are in hot demand, but simply hiring them is not the challenge. A winning digital team needs the right developers. I'll argue that what you're looking for in a developer is not background in certain languages or tasks. Instead, what you need is a sense of curiosity. You're looking for someone who loves the puzzle. You're looking for someone who approaches that puzzle not by examining the pieces but by thinking of the larger systems that hold it. Seeking an individual with a specific talent in one task or another is thinking too short-term for the fast-moving digital world. Whatever they may have perfected at a previous job may well be old hat by the time they walk in your door. You want a developer who is comfortable with the constant reinvention of their skill set. Amit Aggarwal, whom we met earlier in the book, believes that rate of change has totally altered the DNA of successful developers. He believes that given the rate of fundamental change, "specific skill sets don't matter." That's a big deal. Historically there have been Java developers, .Net developers, front-end developers, and full-stack developers. Certainly, training counts. But curiosity counts more.

For example, let's look at the rise of artificial intelligence. Thirty years ago AI was the province of academics. Five years ago more and more teams started to hire developers to build AI-based systems. And then came Amazon . . . and Google . . . and Microsoft. As the big clouds started to commoditize AI in the form of application programming interfaces that could be consumed, developers no longer needed to be model-building experts. They needed to rewire their work to take advantage of all the available open-source and cloud APIs. The winning digital team needs developers who find that exhilarating, not daunting—because whatever you hire them to do this year will surely evolve next year.

Gone are the days when product told developers what to do and developers just built it. Certainly there needs to be a division of responsibility between the definers (product managers) and the builders (developers). But great developers want and should have a stake in product definition, just as product managers co-own execution choices with development teams.

Unlike in sales or marketing, where a high-quality team member can improve outcomes by 50 percent or even 100 percent, great development team members can alter outcomes tenfold. That's why more and more winning organizations don't just optimize development teams for cost. They look for the right people, wherever they can be found.

DATA SCIENTIST

Data has changed everything—so much so that many winning organizations have embraced data science as a critical role in most teams. The role of data science didn't even exist until recently—at least not under that title. In the early days of digital, data scientists were mathematicians or statisticians, creating the algorithms and driving the science-based thinking of many companies. They were the academics that you ignored. Data scientist is a title that emerged as the value of that thinking became prominent.

As an example, we can look at Bloomreach's own Samit Paul, who leads our data science team. He has a long history of working with data-intensive technology businesses, including American Express, Yodlee, and Intuit. With so much data present everywhere, it's essential to have someone who can make sense of it and draw the right conclusions. A great data science function can work with designers to develop hypotheses around what the seeker is seeking and work with product managers to optimize the product once it's in the wild. If the currency of designers is creative visualization, that of data scientists is the models that fit the data. But as Samit rightly points out, a strong mathematical orientation and command of the latest data science models are necessary but insufficient conditions for success. So many organizations place data science teams off to the side, simply there to provide advice to executives.

That's a mistake. At Bloomreach, Samit and his data science team are deeply integrated into our product and engineering functions. You'll find the same thing at Google and Facebook. Indeed, modern data scientists are expected to know how to code. They understand the production implications of their models and work closely with development teams to ensure that the algorithms actually work at scale when they hit production. Should the team be using Spark or Kafka? Data scientists should have an opinion. Samit describes the highly integrated nature of data science and engineering at Bloomreach (a growth stage software business) as a key distinction with the setup he found at American Express (a large financial institution), where data science and engineering were more independent of each other.

Data science in the digital team means the product speaks data. Data science outside the digital team means that executives set up meetings every so often to hear the insights of their data scientists—and then get back to regularly scheduled programming.

While great data scientists and great engineers have a lot in common, there are also key distinctions. In the data scientist role, you're looking for an exploratory mindset. While so many great engineers can solve the hardest problems in the world, great data scientists spend their time exploring what problems would be most worth solving. That means diving down rabbit holes from time to time and being willing to acknowledge that data science projects follow winding paths. At Bloomreach, so many of our innovations have been grounded in these explorations. We investigate why certain parts of our ranking algorithms outperform others. We investigate interesting ways to extract meaning out from unstructured documents. At Amit Aggarwal's fashion marketplace, The Yes, building a composite data-driven view of the style of the shopper is at the heart of the data science IP that his team is building.

So many data science projects and teams are not provided enough business context to operate effectively. "Fundamentally," Samit says, "what has remained unchanged over the last twenty years is problem solving. You have a business problem in hand. You need to understand your data and come up with problems and solutions."

Well said.

MERCHANDISING AND OPERATIONS

The rubber meets the road when your real product (or service) meets the customer. That's where merchandising and site operations steps in. This role is called many things—often different by vertical. In retail, it is frequently called merchandising. In B2B, it can be called category management. In other areas, it might be called operations. Bottom line, it is the person who is responsible for ensuring that the right physical product meets the right customer in the digital experience.

To best understand the tremendous evolution of merchandising, we need to take a step back into the history of retail. For so many years, merchants were the heart of retail. They sourced and bought product. If they bought the right product, the retailer would thrive. If not, a lot would be sitting on the shelves. Mickey Drexler spent time in some of the United States' most well-known retailers—Macy's, J.Crew, Ann Taylor, and Bloomingdale's. But he is famous for transforming Gap brands in the 1990s from a relatively small chain to the behemoth that today includes Gap, Gap Kids, Banana Republic, and Old Navy. The company became an iconic part of pop culture and was famous for "khakis, basics and casual Fridays." Mickey was the merchant of merchants.

But what happens in a world where Zara, H&M, and other fast-fashion brands quickly take styles that are working and source them in China in a matter of days or weeks? What happens when Zappos innovates in shoes and improves returns? What happens when fashion marketplaces like Farfetch and the upstart Amit Aggarwal and Julie Bornstein launched, The Yes, make every brand imaginable discoverable online? The playing field shifts from merchandising to site or digital merchandising. Site or digital merchandising is so named because its older cousin, store merchandising, was involved in figuring out how to lay products out in the store. Store merchandisers are the ones you can blame for making sure you have to walk all the way to the back of the store for the pharmacy, ensuring you pick up something else on the round-trip journey. Online that role becomes a critical part of the digital team—site merchandisers ensure that once the product is sourced, the right product is presented to the digital buyer. In B2B, they ensure that each buyer has a unique personalized experience that is on point with what they are looking for, even when there may be multiple categories of buyers, perhaps for pharmaceutical customers and government customers.

For the sake of example, let's dive into the world of site merchandisers, though the evolution of the role we see there applies to their cousins in operations or category management. Site merchandising has been around since e-commerce has been around, but it has largely been an operational pursuit. It has been about loading SKUs into digital systems and ensuring that the products are described correctly and that the right technology is used to make the digital shopping experience frictionless.

But as is the case for all critical team roles, data and technology have changed everything. Salee Suwansawad has spent thirteen years at Old Navy as a merchant coordinator and now site manager. She is the site merchant for oldnavy.com. She remembers that data had always been at the heart of digital and site merchandising, but that mostly meant digging through historical sales of products and ensuring that next season's lineup, when presented digitally, benefited from that learning. But now she is in the business of using analytics tools, like those provided by Bloomreach and a number of other vendors, to optimize the site experience. She believes in algorithms and data. She knows that she simply cannot merchandise the site for millions of visitors and hundreds of thousands of products.

Salee also knows the limitations of the technology and can talk about how the systems don't permit merchandising "nine-digit colorways" just yet. Great site merchandisers aren't threatened by automation—they welcome it. They know that getting exactly the right product to the right customer in the moment of truth is the heart of a great digital experience. And they want all the help they can get so they can spend less time fixing what is broken on the website and more time optimizing the category for growth and performance.

Everything that changes in a business ultimately comes through the digital experience. And that road goes through the operations functions. Like so many with operations functions, site merchandisers and category managers can be inundated. They launch new products digitally. They retire old ones. They prune the assortment. They may edit the content and the copy around those offerings. They promote the right offering for Christmas. They do whatever it takes.

Like that of your CDO, this role is best discovered at a crossroads—in this case, the intersection of merchandise and technology. That's a mash-up you're less and less likely to find in the aisles of a brick-and-mortar store.

That wasn't always the case. Early e-commerce was often staffed with crossovers from the "real" stores. But the more expansive the digital possibilities, the less likely a store star can make the leap to a digital star. A winning merchandiser today is more likely to come up in digital rather than retail.

Salee, a graduate of The Fashion Institute of Design & Merchandising, has seen that in her own experience at Gap and its division, Old Navy. When she hires now, she's looking less for fashion sense and more for facility with data. That's a reflection of the way a digital experience differs from a live one. Merchandising used to be a visual skill, she says. Now it's about operationalizing data science. She hasn't let go of storytelling. Great brands have a point of view, and they balance between listening to the data and guiding the customer to the answer. Like so many of our digital functions, merchandising and site operations has become an interdisciplinary pursuit.

MARKETING

So much has changed in digital marketing that it's hard to remember what it used to be like. What we know is that the success or failure of your digital endeavors hinges on great digital marketing.

I knew I had seen a great digital marketer when I first met Robert Chatwani. At the time, he was the CMO of eBay. He had one of the largest digital marketing budgets in the world—and was among Google's largest customers. He later went on to be the CMO of Atlassian, one of the world's most innovative software companies. Robert traces the evolution of digital marketing in three phases—brand, channel, and now cross-channel individualized. In the early days of digital, when Yahoo! was king, impressions of the brand were the ticket to digital relevance. We then went through a "channelification" of digital marketing teams. Larger teams, or smaller teams through their agencies, needed expertise in email, mobile, search (Google), social networking (Facebook and Twitter), visual (Pinterest and Instagram)—and on and on. The digital channel had a ton of nuances, and optimizing each channel for growth and efficiency was the key to success.

But to win big in today's hypercompetitive digital landscape requires more. It requires a deep understanding of the interplay between the channels. Indeed, the average digital customer will touch a brand on multiple platforms before they buy or engage. Robert says the debate that he remembers having with Meg Whitman in the early days of eBay's marketing has been settled. You need to go where the customer is and combine channel expertise with a deep understanding of the interplay between the channels. This is not theoretical. It's ultimately about allocation of marketing dollars. Robert believes that a great CMO is the "choreographer of all the customer touchpoints." The CMO choreographs the journey and allocates the money dynamically across the channels.

Like those in so many of our previous functions, great digital marketers are cross-trained across the marketing stack. They understand marketing technology, the plethora of tools available to acquire and nurture customers. They understand the principles behind each channel, if not the nitty gritty details. They have a bias to action, primarily by way of a demand generation or campaigns strategy.

In so many organizations, *marketing* and *customer* can be synonymous. In fact, at Atlassian, Robert describes the "community," the rabid developers that advocate for Atlassian's products, as a key to marketing. They have a strong voice. Harnessed well, they advocate for the company. But they can also put Atlassian in a box and must be complemented by efforts to drive awareness in all the new markets that represent growth engines for the company.

With all the highly analytical skills that modern marketers must have, there is still the noise that must be cut through. Indeed, great digital marketing organizations have developed a strong culture of testing everything. That makes sense when the fickle consumer is hard to predict. But testing can sometimes suppress common sense. Not everything is analytical, and marketing needs a humanizing moment. The winning digital team needs a marketing leader who has not given up on the value of human intuition.

Marketing is a function that has been reimagined by digital transformation. It is infused with data science in a way that old Madison Avenue would never recognize. But winners in this space are engaged, not overrun by data. At its core, the decision to engage in a digital experience is not simply a math problem. There is a human element to convincing seekers—humans—to connect with your offering. When asked, Robert, who can talk numbers and return on ad spend with the best of them, will ask, "What's the ROI on your Mom?"

Indeed, great digital marketers can see through the numbers to the truth.

SALES

We've spoken about the core six members of the digital team, but we can't leave the topic of digital teams behind us without covering the people who bring in the money, especially in B2B businesses—salespeople. Sales teams are rarely part of the digital team, but they are such an important customer of the team that in B2B they may as well be on the team.

Key ingredients for the successful sales job used to be steak and wine. Sales leaders practiced their craft over curated social gatherings. Theirs was a position that demanded top interpersonal skills. Often the top deals would be built on the ability of the sales leader to make personal connections with the client. It was a position with a deep level of relationship.

The internet changed the sales function—but not from the sales leader's point of view. The change came in the client. With the advent of digital transformation, a completely different client came to the sales meeting. They arrived fully versed in the product and the pricing and the competition—all of which can be gleaned from internet research. This reality shifts the role of sales. A winning digital team's sales lead is not going into the meeting to tell the customer about the product. Instead, the sales lead is going in there to solve the customer's problem.

Bloomreach's own chief revenue officer, Rob Rosenthal, clearly articulates how much sales in a digital-first world has changed. He has worked his way up the sales ladder and has seen the changes in his function. Relationships are still important to great sales work, he says, but in the digital world, they're hardly the only tool. What does that mean for salespeople? It means that great salespeople are masters at using digital tools. "Why would you not follow an executive on Twitter to see who they are and what they care about?" Rob asks. So much of selling is knowing the customer, and so much about the customer can be learned online.

But selling has mostly changed because buying has changed. B2B buyers do the overwhelming amount of their research before they ever speak to a salesperson. Salespeople have the same feeling that doctors have when the patient walks in asking for a specific medicine they have read about on the internet. Great salespeople have the ability to take that digital knowledge and reframe the business problem in a way that wins the deal. They have the ability to orchestrate the digital journeys of all the many members of a buying constituency—each doing their own research. Ultimately, these salespeople can bring the buying group together around a great solution to a business problem. Indeed, as always, trust is at the heart of the matter. It is just that trust used to be about common backgrounds and steak and wine. Now it's mostly about product and customer knowledge.

Winning sales leaders are quite knowledgeable about the digital tools that have become available to help them run their business. Sales forecasts, systems, activities, and training are all areas that that have been transformed with world-class digital tools and the accompanying data they contain.

The tools are the easy part. Having a digitally native sales team—that's the real key to winning.

THE EXTENDED TEAM

The core digital team is exactly that—the core. But in the concentric circles around the core are all the rest of the teams that make the business run—creative, manufacturing, finance, HR, legal, and so many more. Indeed, while a focused and excellent core team is essential, digital is a fitness program for the whole organization, from the CEO on down. Winning digital teams see their charter in the context of a team sport. The team is only as good as the weakest link, and digital teams see their charter as embracing and shepherding the rest of the organization through the unknowns of their digital journey.

A FINAL TEAM MEMBER: CULTURE

The last element of a winning team isn't a title or a skill set. It's a context. Winning digital teams exist in the right culture.

"Culture eats strategy for breakfast" is a quote allegedly attributed to Peter Drucker. Nowhere is that more true than in transformational digital undertakings. There is a reason that the best technology businesses have strong and well-understood cultures. Because so little is clear and the rate of change is so fast-paced, winning digital organizations understand that they need to be intentional about their cultures.

At the heart of it, digital teams, unlike many other teams in an organization, need to be able to function in highly ambiguous circumstances. Christy Augustine, who is our chief operations officer at Bloomreach, started her career building the first version of search at Walmart.com and spent time at Bain & Co. before she joined us. She describes a key attribute of a Bloomreacher as someone who can "deal with ambiguity." She contrasts that with the well-understood roles she remembers at Walmart. We hear the same message from winning CDOs. John Koryl describes the team member he values most as someone "who can figure it out."

Great digital cultures can also deal with failure—lots of it. So much of the digital journey is uncertain, but risk aversion is a sure-shot way to facilitate being disrupted. So how do so many successful digital leaders deal with failure? Some may celebrate it. At a minimum, they will undertake an objective postmortem and simply move on. Behind every successful digital product company, including Bloomreach, is a long list of failed attempts.

Great cultures are often interdisciplinary. I experienced that first-hand working side by side with John Koryl when he brought a team of fashion experts from Neiman Marcus to Bloomreach to brainstorm how we could build "the mobile experience of the future." We set up a joint hackathon, each of us willing to take the risk that flying several digital fashion experts to Mountain View, California, to collaborate with great data scientists and engineers might result in something interesting. Day one of the hackathon presented cultural challenges—neither side could even understand what the other was talking about. But by day two, the wheels were turning. The dialogue was getting more interesting. The fashion experts and the AI experts were taking turns at the whiteboard. By day three, when John and I returned to the office, we were blown away by the level of innovation that emerged from a cross-pollinated and committed but culturally diverse team. John felt it had the potential to change their business, which at the time was suffering from an increasing number of mobile shoppers who were converting at lower rates. I felt that we could build a new digital product that could lead the market. It turned out that both of us were right.

There is no right answer to what the right cultural values are for a digital team. At Bloomreach, we center on five core values: own, think, we, truth, and no drama. *Own* is about behaving like an owner, knowing that creative and talented employees like to be empowered to make decisions, much as the owner of a business or an organization might. *Think* is about first principles, the strong belief that each individual should come back to their core beliefs and be open to questioning anything. *We* is about recognizing that ours is a team sport, not a star culture. *Truth* is about ensuring that data stays at the forefront in our minds and guides all decisions. Finally, *no drama* is about promoting a team of problem solvers, not politicians.

But it's not what the culture is that matters. It's that the culture drive a high degree of commitment and be genuinely operationalized in the day-to-day work of the team. Sameer Hassan, who is senior vice president of enterprise product strategy and user experience at Williams-Sonoma, attributes much of his company's success in e-commerce to the transformation of the team from "mercenaries to missionaries." The question I ask myself as we roll out a new policy or decision is, Will this decision increase or decrease the level of commitment of the team? All winning can be traced back to the commitment level of a great team.

8

CREATE YOUR MONEY-MAKING ARCHITECTURE

If Silicon Valley has a weakness, it's a tendency to fall in love with a product.

I've seen this happen many times. An entrepreneur with a vision creates an innovative and exciting product and offering—and then stops dead in the business creation process. Innovators are often product geniuses. They imagine and bring forth all manner of mind-blowing things for us—supercomputers that fit in your pocket, marketplaces that span the globe, cameras that fly.

But a winning digital experience is much more than a great product and offering. A winning digital experience is a great product and offering that is housed in a thoughtfully crafted money-making machine. Winners make money. For a product to take off and the digital experience to be a winner, it needs the right architecture around it.

In this chapter, we'll look at the elements of money-making architecture. It is not a one-size-fits-all system. There are decisions to be made and options to review before your digital experience can be up and running in its winning framework.

Table 8.1

Three Business Models for Money-Making Architecture

Transactional model	The e-commerce business model is, at its heart, transactional in nature. The digital business makes money only when the customer buys something, and the price commanded by the product is a function of supply and demand.
Subscription model	In a subscription arrangement, a customer must pay a recurring price at regular intervals for access to a product or service. Tien Tzuo evangelized the shift to subscription-based business models and coined the phrase "subscription economy." At the heart of a subscription-based model is the mantra of the seeker: it's not about the product; it's about what the customer is trying to do. The core concept of subscription is that the customer doesn't necessarily want to own your product or service—just use it.
Consumption model	In a consumption-based business, the customer pays more for the service as they use it more. Why might I want to do that? Metromile offers pay-per-mile auto insurance, closely tying its revenue (and risk) to how much you drive. Why should someone commuting three hours a day pay the same amount for insurance as someone who drives thirty minutes a day when the risks and costs are fundamentally different? Better to tie outcomes to the business model.

TIE YOUR BUSINESS SUCCESS TO THE SEEKER'S SUCCESS

The first beam in money-making architecture is the business model. The best possible business model for a winning digital experience is one that ties the business to a seeker-sought outcome. What do I mean by that? The goal of the business must be aligned with the goal of the seeker. That's harder to find that goal than you may think.

Consider the real estate business. Your goal as a home buyer is to buy a home for the lowest price possible. But the business is set up in such a way that you almost always have to use a real estate agent. And real estate agents are paid a commission based on the home price. So your goals are not just not aligned—they're in conflict. You want a low price, but the real estate agent wants a high one. The business of real estate lacks a seeker-centric outcome. It's ripe for a seeker-centric makeover, as we've seen my friend Alex Rampell note in his discussion of his real estate businesses.

The outcome-based model is the best possible arrangement for a seeker. Think about shared-ride services. I want to get from point A to point B efficiently. Uber makes money on the same outcome. We are aligned. Here's another: Streetline makes sensors that offer real-time parking availability and parking demand data. If I'm driving in Los Angeles, I want a parking space near my destination, and I do not want to spend half an hour circling the neighborhood hoping to get lucky. Furthermore, the city would like me to park and pay for that spot and quit spewing unnecessary smog into the atmosphere. We are aligned in our desired outcomes—my parked car. Streetline has created a model based on that shared goal.

The model can be taken one step further by aligning the business goals with the ever-increasing happiness of the customer. Get me from point A to point B, and I pay you. Get me there faster and safely, and I pay you even more. Now the business is incentivized to invest even more effort in the seeker's desired outcome because it can realize more money. Outcomes move from aligned to superaligned.

I've seen three distinct kinds of outcome-based business models—transactional, subscription, and consumption. Let's look at all three.

The Transactional Model

The transactional model is the most common. Transactional business models built great businesses like Amazon.com and Google. We know Amazon makes money the way so many e-commerce businesses make money—by selling more things to more people. The e-commerce business model is, at its heart, transactional in nature. The digital business makes money only when the customer buys something, and the price commanded by the product is a function of supply and demand. Less understood is the power of Amazon Marketplace, the program in which third-party sellers offer their wares to the vast Amazon customer base. These days you are more likely to be buying a product *on* Amazon than you are *from* Amazon. Amazon also makes a lot more money on those purchases, taking a clean margin off of third-party sales—and charging fulfillment and shipping fees. While Amazon does not specifically break out its Marketplace profitability, we know it is a significant driver of the company's profit growth. The business model is powerful because from a seller's point of view, you pay Amazon (outside of baseline fees) only when a customer buys your product.

Another example of this model can be seen in Google. Google's powerful cost-per-click advertising, pioneered almost twenty years ago, has been among the most successful transactional business models ever invented. Prior to Google, search business models were driven by CPM (cost per thousand) models where advertisers would pay based on impressions. But impressions tell us very little about genuine intent to buy. The CPC (cost per click) model would charge only if you clicked through from your search on Google to a website. An advertiser could vary its bid based on the conversion rate of that click and its target profitability.

The more people came to Google, the more they clicked on ads, which in turn drove revenue for advertisers and corresponding revenue for Google.

Transactional business models are found everywhere among behemoth winning experiences: Uber's is tied to the number of rides taken and the average price of that ride. PayPal makes its money taking a cut of all the transactions it processes on its two-sided network.

So what's the difference between your run-of-the-mill transactional business model (like traditional e-commerce) and a true outcome-based transactional business model? The difference lies in whether the outcome desired by the funding source is closely tied to the way they pay. In traditional e-commerce, the payer is the customer, who has absolutely no reason to pay a cent more for the product or service they want than they have to. In an outcome-based transactional business model, the incentive structure is very different. As a consumer, I'm open to paying more for "surge pricing" on Uber or for longer journeys because I understand that my price is a function of demand. As a third-party seller on Amazon, I am willing to pay more if I can acquire more customers faster. And as an advertiser on Google, I'm willing to pay more for those keywords that convert at a higher level on my website. In all three cases, my willingness to pay for the offering is closely tied to the outcomes I desire.

The Subscription Model

For the digital business that wants to win big but can't quite fit into a transactional business model, the next option is a subscription-based model. In a subscription arrangement, a customer must pay a recurring price at regular intervals for access to a product or service. Tien Tzuo evangelized the shift to subscription-based business models and coined the phrase "subscription economy." At the heart of a subscription-based model is the mantra of the seeker: it's not about the product; it's about what the customer is trying to do. The core concept of subscription is that the customer doesn't necessarily want to own your product or service—just use it.

As an example, let's look at the contrast between Blockbuster and Netflix. In their early rivalry, these two had the same business model—the renting of entertainment for a fixed price. It was Netflix, however, that had the experience epiphany and applied it to its business model. The original video rental model heavily emphasized choice. But not every visitor to a store or site was in customer mode—ready and able to make a purchase. Instead, they were often in seeker mode—on the hunt for something entertaining. Blockbuster clung to its rental model right into oblivion. Meanwhile, Netflix adapted—shifting to a subscription model, understanding that movie watching is a habit, one in which the seeker doesn't want to be limited. The company understood that the more personalized its recommendations were, the less work you would have to do, the more movies you would want to watch, and the more you would recommend the subscription to a friend. For anyone who ever walked into Blockbuster, wandered the aisles hoping to land on something interesting, and walked out with a copy of *Star Wars* (again) because nothing else looked that good, the offer of a subscription-driven experience was hugely appealing. One company survived. The other became a footnote in business history. The difference was not a tweak in marketing or messaging but a fundamental reorientation of the business model.

Tien notes that millennials increasingly want digital services on demand and for rent. They don't own DVDs—they subscribe to entertainment. They don't just buy pet food; they also subscribe to services like collar tracking and wellness monitoring. And they may sign up for subscription courses on platforms like Udemy and rent textbooks on Chegg. By shrugging off the notion that the customer is an endpoint, subscription economy businesses reorient their behavior to consider the "why" versus the "what" of any transaction and transform their relationships from one-time purchases to recurring subscriptions.

The subscription business model is fundamentally outcome based because seekers can routinely evaluate how happy they are with the product or service. If I'm happy after year one, I'll sign up for year two. That fact sets in motion a virtuous circle of alignment between the consumer and the business. I have to keep serving you better than the competition, or I lose you.

There are benefits to the business and not just the customer in a subscription model—we see this every day at Bloomreach, as this is the business model we've chosen. We are a software-as-a-service (SAAS) business. We have to earn our customer's business every day. But at the same time, our subscription model allows us visibility of our revenue every month. We don't start from zero every day. If we were the legacy sort of software business, we'd sell our software and move along to start from zero with the next customer. Instead, every day we have the opportunity to build on our base. That gives us more visibility to invest. I can plan my cash flows. I can invest accordingly. And I can make you more successful in the process. SAAS businesses have shown the ability to create incredible economic value. They provide the kind of predictability that investors love while at the same time providing the kind of alignment with outcomes that customers love. But the key to a SAAS model is aligning the basis for the subscription with a unit of value that provides for price variance across the target customer base. At Bloomreach, we have historically priced on the metrics of page views and catalog size. The more traffic you have to your website or the larger your product or content catalog, the more we'll charge you. Of course, if you sell more products and have more people visiting your digital properties, you'll also get disproportionately more value from our solution. The subscription unit and the customer outcome are tightly tied.

But you don't have to be selling software to benefit from the subscription model. Apple, whose heart has always been in building beautiful computing machines, has recently focused heavily on subscription-based services, including iCloud (subscribing to storage), Apple Music (subscribing to music), Apple TV+ (subscribing to entertainment), and AppleCare (subscribing to support). That focus is clearly paying off, as Apple CEO Tim Cook has confirmed that Apple will double its services revenue from 2016 to 2020, already past $11 billion per quarter.

The Consumption Model

A consumption-based business model is the third outcome-based option. In a consumption-based business, the customer pays more for the service as they use it more. Why might I want to do that? Metromile offers pay-per-mile auto insurance, closely tying its revenue (and risk) to how much you drive. Why should someone commuting three hours a day pay the same amount for insurance as someone who drives thirty minutes a day when the risks and costs are fundamentally different? Better to tie outcomes to the business model.

The Metromile story reveals an important lesson. While all three business models can be outcome based, the relevant question is this: What outcome does the customer seek? In the case of car insurance, the seeker wants an affordable insurance product that matches their risk profile—proxied by driving frequency. Interestingly auto insurance has historically been a subscription service—I typically pay a fixed amount that is a function of my age and driving history. But Metromile had the insight that a subscription model that did not factor in use or consumption would not match the seeker's intent. Indeed, where subscriptions may fail us, consumption can be a better conduit to align outcomes.

The most famous consumption models are the cloud services offered by the large clouds—Amazon Web Services, Google Cloud Platform, and Microsoft Azure. At the heart of cloud-based innovation is the notion that I pay only for what I use. As a developer getting on one of the platforms at a time when I have no idea how much computing capacity I might need, I can swipe a credit card and simply pay for use. That proposition is highly attractive. Of course, downstream, as usage skyrockets, we yearn for fixed fees. But the clouds have already trained us to expect to pay more for use. Airlines and telecom service providers have used usage-based pricing models for a long time. The more bandwidth or minutes I use, the more I pay. The more I fly, the more I pay. But digital can and has created innovation in those models. Before rolling out the Xfinity service, Comcast always charged a fixed subscription for cable. But the emergence of on-demand content has enabled the cable provider to add a consumption-based dimension to its business model. Now Comcast has the incentive both to upgrade you to the new tier of subscription and to make it easy for you to order your next movie on demand. Both levers have an outcome orientation, and digital has enabled Comcast to add a new dimension for growth—even without acquiring more subscribers. Charging for consumption is valuable only if consumption grows naturally. If, as is the case for on-demand entertainment, the more I use it, the more I will use it in the future, consumption is a winner.

Each of these business models has its pros and cons; there is no single right answer. It starts, as it always does, with understanding the seeker and defining an offering that achieves the outcomes sought by that seeker. From there, the choice of business model flows, and often there are patterns. Transactional business models are often supported by two-sided marketplaces. Subscription-based business models often rely on low marginal costs (like software), the existence of a clear long-term relationship, and cases where the seeker values predictability of spend. Consumption-based business models often have the opposite characteristics. They work when the unit of consumption is superclear—the number of application programming interface calls, minutes, or miles driven. They are often the right choice when the buyer simply doesn't know how much they will use and values the pay-per-use paradigm.

Now what about businesses that don't seem to fit these three models. What can you do about them? Say you're selling cruises. You can't price on outcome because your outcome (booking a cruise) is not the same as the customer's outcome (having a memorable vacation). There's no alignment there. And subscription doesn't make sense either. Some people are avid cruisers, but many will take one, maybe two, in their entire lives. They aren't interested in paying routinely for a twice-in-a-lifetime event. I could charge per cruise booked. So I can't charge on the outcome because we won't agree on what makes a good cruise, and I can't charge a subscription because you're not going on a cruise per month, and while I can (and do) charge on consumption, it's not clear that if I go on a cruise, I'm more likely to go on a second cruise. In fact, the reverse may be true: I may have checked it off the bucket list.

What do I do then?

You need to ask the fundamental question: Is your offering seeker centric? If you can't fit it into an outcome-based model, the problem may not be with your business model. It may be with your offering. Cruises are a good example of this. If what you are offering is an episodic purchase, then perhaps you are simply a commodity provider of cruises. Your offering is not seeker centric. It is differentiated on price or service.

Can you (should you?) look for a way to make this seeker centric? If you're having trouble fitting into the seeker-centric model, you may be asking the wrong question.

Look at your customer and ask "Why are you here?"

If you're the cruise provider and you consider why your customer comes to you, perhaps the answer is to have a romantic vacation. To achieve a seeker-centric business, could you shift your offering? Expand to offer not just cruises but all manner of romantic vacations? Then perhaps instead of doing business with you once in a lifetime, your customer is interested in regular interaction with a company that understands their goal of regular time away. Considering the seeker viewpoint can give you an entirely new outlook on the shape of your day-to-day business.

MARKET THE EXPERIENCE, NOT THE AD

Alongside your model, the next beam to place in your architecture is the marketing strategy. The job of marketing in the age of digital business is to figure out how to acquire more customers and grow at a fraction of the lifetime value of the customer. How do winners do that?

They start by building marketing into the offering itself. Consider the example of Atlassian, the innovative software pioneer of Jira. Jira is a system of record and project management for developers and support teams—so many of the tickets filed to improve software are recorded in Jira. In 2015, Atlassian was generating $70 million per quarter. In the first quarter of 2020, it was making $400 million per quarter. It has 125,000 customers—not bad for a bootstrapped Australian software company. And all this, in its period of rapid growth, with very limited marketing. Atlassian was maniacally focused in its early days on developers—and later on the teams around the developers. Of course, built into Jira was the secret weapon: once one developer was on it, the whole team needed it—natural virality. What's more, Atlassian looks for ways to let its product do the marketing by dropping the barriers between potential customers and the software itself. For example, a new visitor to the Atlassian site will not be asked to register an email to proceed. That's the opposite of how most companies behave. Capturing an email is considered Sales 101. But Robert Chatwani, chief marketing officer of Atlassian, takes a different view. The ask for an email is "creating a gate," he says. It's friction that slows the potential customer from falling in love with the product, he says. The goal of the site is to "get you to the product as fast as possible"—and then let the great product do the customer acquisition work for you.

The marketing strategy must then turn to the topic of channels—which ones to tap and how best to use them. Early digital marketers followed a pretty straightforward formula. Once a website or app was built, they would undertake a set of optimizations to acquire some traffic for free via search engine optimization (SEO) and then seek to acquire customers by bidding for keywords on Google. The idea was to bid less on Google than the value of the conversion event on your website so that you wouldn't be too far in the red as soon as you acquired the customer. The trouble is, of course, that Google ads are an auction, so your bid price is likely to end up at the level the greatest fool in the marketplace is willing to pay. Over time, Google ads start to become less and less profitable without significant optimization.

SEO tactics have also started to work less and less as Google increasingly takes over the search result page with more ads, more owned experiences, and more content that keeps searchers on Google. Facebook offered a contrasting approach: enabling digital marketers to acquire customers based on their likes, their demographics, and a much deeper understanding of their profile. If Google is about intent, Facebook is about the individual. But it suffers from the same challenges. Facebook ads are just a different form of auction, and all its incentives are to keep the user on Facebook, not to build long-term loyalty for the brand.

So what do winning digital marketers do?

While they use all the channels available to them, winning digital marketers take matters into their own hands. They don't view the customer as a transactional entity that has come from Facebook or Google or an email system and somehow landed up on a digital property. Instead, they see the entire digital experience's job as delivering what the arriving individual is seeking. That means deep personalization so that each of us gets a unique experience. It means optimizing the pathways through the digital experience so that each one is frictionless. It means ensuring that calls to action are well placed and the user experience is modern and flawless. If the early days of digital marketing were mostly about optimizing what happens outside your website or app to get people in the door cost effectively, winners today spend as much or more time optimizing what happens when you come in the door. The benefits of analytically focusing on the owned experience are multiplicative. Each one of the digital campaigns starts performing better when conversion rates on the experience improve. The criticality of having a great digital experience standing behind the marketing has fed the wave to adopt digital experience platforms, which, if they do their job right, ensure that marketers can innovate without a reliance on IT.

Winning digital marketers do not think transactionally. They want to acquire the customer only once. They want to pay Google or Facebook only once. They do not want to keep reacquiring that customer over and over. Instead, once the customer has arrived on a brand's digital property, they want to drive them to a sign-up flow so that they can market directly to that customer on an email address or mobile number without the help of Google or Facebook. As an example, fashion marketplace The Yes is available only on a mobile app. This means that to use it, a shopper must create an account and download the app. Sure, that might add friction up front to the customer acquisition process, but The Yes has clearly decided that it is more important to deeply know its customer through a profile they fill out than it is to acquire and reacquire the same customer over and over again through a typical web flow.

While not all digital experience winners choose to go app-only, many will create distinctive value to separate the signed-in users from the general browsers. Visit the onepeloton.com website run by Peloton, and you will see a high-quality shopping experience. But once you sign in, you get the personalized scorecards, classes, and other content recommendations that build with use. In fact, we are increasingly living in a first-party data world to drive personalization. As data privacy boundaries have grown, winning brands understand that deeply knowing who their customers are and what their current intent represents is mission critical to marketing. Connecting the dots between that profile and all marketing activities will come to be expected by all consumers. After all, in this age of authentic communication, nothing is less authentic than speaking to me as a customer in a way that ignores who I am and my last interaction with your brand.

Remember as you're building out your strategy that great marketing doesn't stop and start with the analytical. The right side of the brain is still critical to marketing. Let's return to that onepeloton.com website. It doesn't immediately showcase the products as soon as we arrive there. Instead, it starts with beautiful imagery that evokes its brand values—energy, activism, and inspiration. In a world of cluttered messages, great brands ensure their marketing is memorable. But being memorable isn't just about presenting beautiful imagery and videos; it is also about bringing together content and products in highly unique experiences. We see this with the Bloomreach customer Hobbycraft, which is a leading provider of products for crafts and hobbies in the UK. The Hobbycraft team built a section of their e-commerce experience called "Ideas," which presents the kinds of projects you could undertake with the company's products. For example, "How to Make a Father's Day Card" will list out the steps needed to create a card while alongside featuring the Hobbycraft products that one might need for that card. It is a seamless example of "content and commerce," where Hobbycraft has gone to the seeker's intent (doing a crafting project) to build a winning experience that combines helpful content with associated products.

Of course, that kind of unique experience helps seekers achieve their desired outcomes, but it also helps marketers acquire those seekers before they are ready to buy. Imagine arriving at that Hobbycraft site when you are thinking about the project rather than after having decided what to buy for it. Now Hobbycraft isn't paying Google to acquire the customer at the moment of purchase. It is nurturing that customer toward the purchase naturally. That's winning digital marketing.

WIN BIGGER AS YOU GET BIGGER

What happens when you grow? It's a question the eager entrepreneur may fail to consider up front and, in doing so, may miss out on a critical step in the creation of their money-making architecture. Thinking ahead to the day when you outgrow your one-room offices, your first round of funding, and your initial vision is a critical step toward winning.

For that reason, even at the earliest stages, think about it. How do you make even more money as you scale up? Traditional business schools teach us to think about economies of scale, which mostly come down to sourcing from your suppliers at a lower marginal cost than you used to—leveraging your purchasing power for better deals. But winning digital experiences enable brands to go far beyond that.

As well described in Jim Collins's book *Good to Great*, winning businesses ultimately create great flywheels that increase in velocity as they grow. How is that done?

Build a Platform

Bloomreach focuses much of its customer acquisition on driving great digital experiences for large commerce businesses. We now power brands representing 25 percent of retail e-commerce in the United States and the UK. By acquiring more commerce customers, our platform gains more data, which in turn provides the fuel our artificial intelligence (AI) engine needs to perform better. By performing better, we can drive more revenue and other business outcomes for those customers. We monetize that growth with a series of modular applications: everything from search to personalization to content to analytics to SEO to enabling buy-online/pick-up-in-store. As our customers pay us more money, we invest that in marketing and thought leadership, which in turn causes key systems integration and technology partners to make more money on the platform. They in turn bring us more potential customers. The flywheel now spins just a little bit faster. Key to the Bloomreach flywheel is the data asset we build as we acquire more and more customers. We all see the power of the data network effect in spades when we search on Google. At this point, the software powering Google and the software powering Microsoft's search engine, Bing, may not be all that different. And yet, so many years later, Google is still dominant. Some of that has to do with brand and user habits. But a big part of that is the enormous data asset Google has accumulated in search behavior. There is a really good chance Google knows exactly what you mean when you type something into the search bar—because Google has probably seen it before.

Next plc offers another good example of the flywheel in action. Next is among the most innovative fashion retailers in Europe. Simon Wolfson, its CEO, and Kash Mahmood, who runs its digital team, have consistently pushed the envelope on applications of AI for e-commerce. But the members of the management team at Next wanted to go further. They didn't just want their powerful platform to help their own customers; they wanted it to help the many brands that want to build their own direct-to-customer digital franchises. Next announced Total Platform—a service that would enable brands to run on Next's technology, warehousing, and logistics platform while controlling their own brand, creative, and product experiences. Next would receive a fixed percentage of sales for any services it provided. It is Next's "Amazon Web Services" moment. Just as Jeff Bezos decided to turn his huge infrastructure spend into a money-making asset, Next is taking its unique assets and turning them into a platform for flywheel growth.

Craft Your Ecosystem

Another critical element in money-making architecture is the ecosystem. This is the network of businesses and resources around you that will intersect with your product and elevate it to an experience that delights the seeker.

Creation of an ecosystem starts with a map of all your adjacent markets. This is the way PillPack, an online pharmacy, built its effort. The company began as a packaging concept: What if all your pills could arrive at your doorstep packaged for daily use? You'd just open the pack with today's date—no counting, no worrying about forgetting a dose. The packaging helps you keep track.

From that initial concept, the creators then built an ecosystem around their packaging idea. They created relationships with entities such as pharmacy benefit managers, health insurers, and pharmaceutical distributors. They essentially built a pharmaceutical ecosystem. And this is the power of their offering. The seeker doesn't necessarily want a packaging solution. The seeker just wants help making sure they have the right Rx at the right time in the right dosage. PillPack's ecosystem meets that seeker need.

The truth is that a winning digital business will likely sell at lot more than it alone can provide. The most important thing you could be doing is fostering deep integrations with your ecosystem to deliver on the offerings because the probability is relatively low that you alone encompass more than a small part of the total offering that you need to deliver to satisfy a seeker. You can generate the opportunity; the value you're providing is the ability to connect with the seeker and say "I understand what you need. I'm going to help you." But after that, you'll likely need partners to make it all happen. Simply handing the seeker off to a partner is not a good long-term strategy. You need to be in a position to guarantee that all the ecosystem partners will work together in harmony. You have to take responsibility for the aggregate service you offer.

When you do take on this responsibility, the potential for creating a loyal customer and making a lot more money jumps. Any digital business needs its allies. Each of those ecosystem partners is a potential ally. Done right, they will all be selling, marketing, supporting, and innovating on your digital business. Imagine the multiplicative effect. It is not just technology companies that can build technology ecosystems. I saw this firsthand through our relationship with FC Bayern Munich, the powerhouse soccer team based in Munich. Bayern announced a series of "hack days" in Allianz Arena, its beautiful stadium. Developers from around Europe could come together to build incredible applications on the Bayern platform. We at Bloomreach participated in one of the hack days, and out of it came incredible applications in the areas of personalized fan experiences, virtual and augmented reality, and global networking, among others. So much innovation was delivered by the ecosystem—all in a way that gains Bayern more passionate fans and helps it make more money.

The Two-Sided Solution

Platform, ecosystem, and data network effects all help winning digital businesses make more money as they grow, but perhaps the most powerful type of network effect multiplier comes from two-sided marketplaces. We see them everywhere. We discussed the Amazon Marketplace earlier in this chapter. We've seen it with PayPal:

The more consumers use PayPal to pay, the more merchants it acquires. And the more merchants it acquires, the more consumers become interested in using the service. Two-sided marketplaces can create winners. Consider Olo, a mobile and online food-ordering platform that allows customers to order food from online menus and prepay from their mobile or desktop device. It is a company with two distinct, yet related seekers: it serves both the hungry, time-pressed consumer and the chain restaurant worried about losing its customers to virtual disruptors. Olo works with restaurants to create mobile applications for smartphones as well as mobile-optimized ordering websites. The apps are integrated with the restaurant's point-of-sale systems. Olo's genius is that it brings two parties together in an efficient, seamless way, allowing both to achieve their goals. David Frankel was an early investor in Olo (and PillPack) and saw the two-sided marketplace potential. Restaurants could retain their customers, and customers could order and pay with ease. No matter which side of the transaction you're on, "they need you as much as you need them," David says.

KEEP SCORE IN A NEW WAY

The final beam in your architecture is what you might think of as the finish line. Winners have to cross the finish line to claim their prize. How do you know where that line is and when you've reached it? In a footrace, you break the ribbon. In business, you set up a new type of measurement system.

As businesses increasingly move to make money in new ways, they must keep score in a new way. We have all grown up in a world where we are trying to optimize for EBITDA. The theory is that the more we can improve our customer satisfaction or the efficiency with which a customer can buy our products and services, the more we can increase the top line or reduce costs—both in service of EBITDA growth. The trouble is that this line of thinking may optimize EBITDA in the short term, but it will not anticipate the likely disruption that may come from a seeker substituting our products with a full experience that caters to their higher-order intention.

Winning digital businesses will measure themselves with a different yardstick: the lifetime value of a customer. The seeker-centric business will focus on the unit economics of its customer: How often do they come back? How much of their basket of purchases do they make from us? What holds back the adoption of our product or service in their life? These signals will tell us the long-term value of the customer to our business and enable us to make investments against that long-term value. Our own business, Bloomreach, is a subscription-based software business. The key metric for us is the lifetime value of our customer—impacted by our annual recurring revenue from that customer, the length of time we anticipate them being with us, the growth of that relationship, and our cost to serve them. Optimizing for lifetime value is what allows Netflix to offer a seemingly affordable subscription service. The company knows it may take many months or even a year to pay back its cost of acquiring you as a customer, but it also knows that by treating you as a seeker of regular entertainment, it's got you hooked for a long time. Your value to Netflix well exceeds its near-term costs, a conclusion it could never reach by optimizing for short-term EBITDA.

SPEND MONEY TO MAKE MONEY

Everything we've discussed in this chapter—innovating on the business model, building ecosystems or platforms, and marketing in a highly personalized manner, all while keeping score for the long term—can be expensive. This is not the kind of operation started on maxed-out credit cards in the family garage. It may take a good amount of capital to make the offering and the model work. In most winning digital experiences, it comes down to a simple fact: you will likely make less money up front in these models in return for the promise that you will make a lot more over time. Lifetime value thinking can be a competitive weapon. It's a bit like investing in a real estate project. Getting your money back is a process that plays out over time. There's a reason Bloomreach needed over $100 million in capital and Amazon still nets less than a 5 percent margin. Winning big requires big bets. But the real question is, Do you want to die a slow death, or do you want to embrace your customers' inner seeker, build what wins them over, and invest to make a lot more money from them in the long run?

Winning digital teams leave sunk costs behind. They embrace the disruptor's mindset and think big. Money isn't everything. But it's how we determine who's winning.

9

THE WINNING B2B EXPERIENCE

A good digital team knows its customer.

In a business-to-consumer (B2C) setting, that customer may have a very distinct persona. Picture the conference room of a digital team in a B2C space. The team might have a description of the typical customer up on the wall. Perhaps she's in her thirties, with a modest disposable income and interests in fitness and fashion. She has a preferred time and place for her commerce activities, and she's happy to provide feedback on her experience. Perhaps her composite image is accompanied by a journey map showing how she wants to buy from you.

Elsewhere in the office complex, we visit the conference room of a business-to-business (B2B) digital team. And if there's any imagery of the target customer up in that conference room, it looks a lot different. Now we're staring at a multiheaded monster, with eyes all over and tentacles swinging every which way. The monster wants something different every moment of the day and is frighteningly rational about where it can go to find what it wants. The image up on the wall is not of one customer but of many, all interacting with your brand but with highly distinct needs and personas.

This is the difference between B2C and B2B digital teams. One can conjure up an image of the target customer and fall in love. The other has a target customer that is the stuff of nightmares.

Indeed, the challenge of B2B is that the customer is not a he, she, or they. It's an it: an organization or business that may have many humans within it but none the team can count on to be the sole point of contact. A B2B digital experience may have one company as a "customer," but under that heading comes a wide variety of users. The site may be accessed in the morning by a scientist with a PhD, in the afternoon by a shop steward with vocational training, and in between by the summer intern who isn't sure what he's doing one minute to the next. The site may be functioning in one instance as a purchasing portal and the next as a research tool. It's no wonder that B2B sellers find the digital experience daunting. While their B2C brethren are carefully curating their target customer, B2B is faced with a hydra.

How do you build a highly personalized, unique digital experience when your customer is not a person? That's the dilemma we face in this chapter.

To start with, if you're like 60 percent of B2B manufacturers and 38 percent of B2B wholesalers, you mostly don't. That's the proportion of B2B organizations that don't even have a basic website. Indeed, B2B e-commerce penetration as a percentage of the total B2B market is about 8 percent. Retail e-commerce penetration is about double that. I fully expect B2B digital experiences to grow faster and start catching up to their B2C brethren. After all, the same human beings who use modern applications for their digital personal lives show up to work only to find that so many of the digital applications they use there are at best clunky and at worst nonexistent. But the fact remains that digital maturity in many B2B businesses lags that of their B2C counterparts. It is essential that B2B teams recognize where their organizations are and chart a realistic path that accounts for the starting point.

Many B2B sellers are fully committed to changing, but the advice offered by experts seems somewhat irrelevant. While much of digital transformation focuses on creating a unique personalized experience, B2B knows that just won't work. At any given business, it's unlikely the user is just one person. Everything that digital experts use to create a personalized experience—tracking clicks and non-clicks, location, time, and previous history—only creates a deeply impersonal picture.

So this question then emerges: Do you need a person to create personalization?

The answer is no. The individual nature of personalization is a fallacy. Personalization, despite its etymology, does not require an individual at the keyboard. It's an experience that can cover everything from one moment for one person to one person's digital journey to an organization's experience. The concept relies not on how many users there are but on what they have in common. Much of the literature on B2B digital experiences has highlighted the need to learn from consumers—the "consumerization of IT." In fact, B2B providers must recognize that while some of the B2C rules apply, others do not. The challenge for them is discerning which is which.

USE THE SEEKER FRAMEWORK

The good news for B2B providers is that the seeker framework we've discussed works in a B2B setting. While the individual human beings in a company may be vastly different in their demographics, they share a seeker identity. They are all entering this digital experience with a business goal in mind. There may not be a single, coherent customer. But there is likely a single profile of a seeker.

Smart B2B firms are already embracing this reality. At first glance, a B2B business may seem incompatible with a B2C personalization process. Steven Baruch is chief strategy and marketing officer of MSC Industrial Direct, a national distributor of metalworking and repair products for manufacturers and a Bloomreach customer. Business customers come to MSC looking for everything from waste-reduction solutions to a new part for a broken lathe. Founded post-WWII by a sole proprietor selling tools out of his car, the company now serves customers that range from multinational aerospace manufacturers to public school maintenance departments.

That means Steve's "customer" has many faces. His users easily span five generations. This makes personalization a Herculean task. Take a simple purchasing decision, he says. A machine is broken and likely needs a new part. The company has long used MSC. What happens next?

If that individual looking for that part is a baby boomer, the answer is simple. They would walk to the bookshelf on the shop floor or perhaps in the office, and they would reach for the 4,500-page, full-color catalog—a publication produced annually by MSC and fondly referred to by all as the "Big Book." The Big Book has been the cornerstone of the MSC sales process for decades, and despite the advent of other forms of commerce, it has a passionate fan base. "I literally have customers who would not let me pry our Big Book from their cold, dead hands," says Steve.

The Big Book user would flip through the catalog, find the necessary part, and take down the order information. He may pick up the phone to place the order or log onto a desktop to visit the website.

Imagine the same scenario, but now the individual tackling the problem of the broken machine part is a relative newcomer to the company—a recent graduate who identifies as Gen Z. This individual wouldn't know what to do with a 4,500-page catalog if it fell on his foot. While other customers swear by the Big Book, this one would think it's literally an offense against nature, killing trees and increasing the company's carbon footprint. "This is the customer who sees the Big Book and wants to have me tarred and feathered in the town square," says Steve.

The idea of paging through a tome that size seems ridiculous. He was likely shown the bookshelf of catalogs on his plant tour on his first day and hasn't noticed it since. When he needs a part, he's immediately on the nearest screen—perhaps a desktop, more likely his phone—and he's searching a digital catalog to find the part and place the order without having any other human interaction.

How can Steve personalize the experience for these two very different people? The answer: don't treat the user as a customer; treat them as a seeker.

In fact, while the two employees may seem very different in their behavior, they share a commonality in their seeker status—which is to get that broken machine up and running again. That creates a unified seeker profile that spans the generations and environmental sensibilities. Steve must embrace the multiple methods his seeker will use, but all of them converge in the same seeker profile. All those channels lead him to one experience.

Whatever their generation, experience, or shopping method of choice, Steve's seeker shares a common set of emotions: a sense of urgency and a need for accuracy.

That's a different mindset than you find in a B2C user, he says. "As an example, at home you might have Glad trash bags on an auto replenishment order. And that's fine. You can keep an extra box in the house. If you're out, you can make a run to the store. Your life is not going to end. But at work, you need to be thinking about production at all times. If you're not doing your job better, cheaper, faster, smarter, somebody else will. So if you're out of something, it's more of an existential problem than an inconvenience." The MSC seeker also needs exactly the right part to fix the machine. A part that almost works may as well not work at all. The seeker needs accuracy.

With that understanding, Steve has his seeker. When his digital experience serves the seeker, the behavior and demographics of the individual user fade into the background for digital designers. The sense of urgency and the need for accuracy are the overreaching elements that connect his disparate users. With these as his guide, the winning digital experience emerges. It's the experience that serves the seeker's sense of urgency, immediately delivering the ability to find the right part and order it.

I've the seen the design points of immediacy and accuracy emerge across our work at Bloomreach powering search for B2B customers. Typical search technology has, for many years, relied on the paradigm of precision and recall. When you search for something, recall gives you all the possible results that match the query, and precision ensures that only the most relevant results are brought forward. The larger the recall set, the harder it is to have high precision.

The higher the precision, the greater the chance you might miss a result from the recall set. Precision and recall are the twin forces that compete with each other for great search.

At their core, so many B2B experiences demand high precision. Whether you are looking to source a power tool from Bosch, replace a part for a water heater from HD Supply, or obtain an Aprilaire 20" x 25" Whole Home Air Purifier Merv 13 from Carrier Enterprise, what's clear is you're looking for something really, really specific. All those Bloomreach customers demand precision. Because of that, delivering a great experience is about getting the seeker to exactly the right part in the shortest time possible. Other brands have approached the accuracy problem in other ways, requiring that the customer track through a tree of categories to navigate to the part rather than enabling free-form search. In effect, they have decided that accuracy is more important than immediacy.

But a great B2B digital experience should not require that trade-off. At Bloomreach, we have solved these kinds of problems with a technology we call semantic understanding. We are able to dis-ambiguate the make, the model, the brand, and the dimensions so that when you look for the perfect part, the digital experience can deliver what you are seeking within milliseconds of you typing a few characters into a search bar.

Let's remember that the Big Book that Steve's baby boomers refer to can be highly efficient. His clients have been using it for years and can instantly thumb to exactly the right part. "Our driver is time," he says. When he can deliver that quality of instant experience and give time back to his seeker, the debates over the fate of the Big Book in the twenty-first century will fade away.

WHAT IF THERE REALLY ARE MULTIPLE SEEKERS?

Unfortunately, not all B2B seeker behavior can be unified into a single digital experience. Imagine you're a large-scale construction company considering a strategic relationship with a power tools provider to standardize the options for your workers. You're considering Bosch power tools versus a competitor like DeWalt. It's a decision that an engineer is going to make on behalf of the construction company to ensure that all its workers are using a standard set of tools. For Bosch, such a contract could be worth a lot of money and usher in a steady stream of revenue for years to come in the form of accessories, warranties, and replenishment orders. The company is keen to win over the engineers considering the decision by highlighting all the latest technology it is bringing to the table, including its new Revolt Core 18V battery, which claims one of the highest cuts-per-charge ratios around. The Bosch digital experience contains great videos, detailed specifications, testimonials from other buyers, and all kinds of other great technical information. The goal of the digital experience is to win over the educated professional who is looking to make a design decision.

Now imagine Bosch gets into commerce, and instead of selling through distributors, it starts selling direct to customers. It will likely have visitors to its digital property who go beyond the "research-oriented professional" who is looking to deeply understand the products and services on offer and what makes them special. Perhaps a maintenance person will be looking to get in and out of the experience with an accessory or to check the status of a repair. How does Bosch deliver a highly personalized experience for two distinct seekers seeking different things?

Personalization and artificial intelligence (AI) can help here—but we must start with the recognition that the entire experience must be different for the researcher than it might be for the maintenance person. Once we know what persona has arrived, the digital experience needs to morph into a highly unique one for that persona; only then can we learn from the behavior of others within that persona. We see a simple version of that kind of experience at the digital property of metal-cutting solution provider Sandvik Coromant. Before even giving you a page to view, the company's website asks you to select the role in which you are visiting from a range of options: production engineer, CAM programmer, purchaser, machine operator, distributor/partner, or other. If I select production engineer, it will then ask me "What brings you to sandvik.coromant.com today?" and offer me more options: find a tool, solve a machining problem, place an order, download a drawing, find cutting data, contact the company, or other. All this before I have even seen the home page. Sandvik has determined that personalization must be directly influenced by organizational role and need. Once I have provided those pieces of information, the website can direct me to a tailored experience that is a lot more personalized.

Bloomreach has taken this kind of personalization to a different level. Once a customer has authenticated—because they have either selected an option like Sandvik offers or logged in—Bloomreach AI can offer segmented ranking, in effect ensuring that every interaction involving a production engineer or machinist from any company informs the interactions with the next individual in the same role. Importantly, the AI needs to understand that the value of every interaction is not the same. Winning the research engineer might result in millions of dollars of value, though they may visit a lot less frequently than the procurement person. Great B2B AI can learn from the crowd—but it must be the right crowd with the right weighting.

The personalization doesn't stop with an experience tailored to a role or need. It can extend to the contractual entitlements of the customer. Among the most common B2B digital needs is the ability to handle custom contracts and custom pricing. Unlike B2C experiences, B2B experiences contain highly unique commercial terms. If you log in on behalf of an organization, it's essential that those unique terms be presented in the experience, much as a salesperson would provide a custom quote for a large customer.

LET REAL LIFE GUIDE DIGITAL LIFE

How can you figure out what a B2B user wants from a digital experience? The answer may lie in the way they interact offline.

Figure 9.1 Staples delivers a virtual business relationship. Shutterstock.

When Faisal Masud arrived to serve as chief digital officer of Staples after stints at great digitally native B2C properties like Amazon and eBay, it was clear to him that the B2B customer was the right target. Already the vast majority of Staples' online customers were small and medium-sized businesses. They were regulars, with big basket sizes and predictable orders. But office products comprise a competitive market, and keeping those customers happy required more than just an online option. It had to be a winning online option.

Faisal's team dug into research about the digital Staples customer. The team members all had ideas about how the experience could be improved. But it was an offline behavior that caught Faisal's eye. Staples customers loved their delivery drivers.

These weren't just any delivery drivers. They were Staples' dedicated fleet. Decades before, Staples founder Tom Steinberg had pioneered the idea of having his own delivery fleet. Even as UPS and FedEx grew, his customers were served by Staples drivers.

And Faisal quickly found this was a relationship that endured. Customers knew their drivers. They trusted them to get products to their businesses on time. They reached out to their drivers to answer questions or to resolve problems. And the drivers returned the loyalty. They knew their routes. They knew the names of the key personnel. They frequently acted as first-line researchers, reporting back to headquarters on the likes and dislikes of the Staples buyer.

This, Faisal realized, was a key element he needed to embrace. The Staples B2B customer wanted a relationship. His map to success was now clear: to serve and expand the Staples B2B relationship, the winning digital experience needed to serve and protect the relationship business customers had already built with the live Staples fleet. "We had built a moat around the business with our fulfillment," he said. The digital experience needed to reflect that truth in order to resonate with B2B users. Visit Staples Advantage, its digital property focused on repeat business customers, and you will see the beginnings of the intuition of people—drivers, salespeople, and account managers—being translated into the online property. Prominently, you will see capabilities that allow repeat business buyers to store their lists to enable easy restocking. Recent purchases are visibly displayed, knowing that so many business buyers reorder the same thing over and over again. Built into the property are spend controls to ensure budgets are not overrun, and systems can be integrated into typical procurement processes. In effect, the digital property aims to make what the human beings would do in the real world a lot easier. All this data is accessible to the sales or account manager. Indeed, personalized service from a human being should be used to delight beyond what the digital experience can deliver scalably and interlaced into an elegant analog-plus-digital experience.

Generating the right analog-plus-digital experience also means ensuring that exactly the right data attributes of complex B2B products are present, accessible, and summarized for buyers. Jason Hein, who joined Bloomreach after twenty years across great B2B companies like McMaster-Carr and Amazon Business, describes a project to digitally market internet protocol cameras. These cameras,

Jason says, have over seventy unique attributes—seventy ways each camera might be different from the others. On the one hand, it's really important for the description of each camera to be highly accurate so that someone looking for something specific can find it easily. On the other hand, it is equally important to be able to highlight the two or three most important distinguishing characteristics of a given camera because someone earlier in the consideration process will be looking for takeaways. Tough task.

DON'T FOLLOW AMAZON

It can be tempting to look at the most successful e-commerce entity in the world and copy that, but much of the "Amazon for Business" offering can lead B2B providers astray.

Amazon.com's appeal, in part, revolves around selection. Vast, like its river namesake, the sheer volume of items for sale is designed to keep the customer within the walls forever. Why would you go anywhere else? Who has more to offer?

That breadth of offering is a decidedly B2C feature. And there is certainly a place for that in B2B. As so many distributors struggle to match the selection, prices, and findability that Amazon offers, more and more millennial purchasing managers don't want to speak to salespeople and want to shop where they always shop—Amazon. That works well for the hundreds of thousands of small businesses whose primary needs look a lot like those of consumers. But chasing Amazon is not a winning path. The selection/price/findability trio is one that Amazon has conquered. The key for B2B winners is to find other ways to win big by catering to different seekers and offering different solutions.

Fortunately the opportunity to stand out remains large. Some of the most successful B2B businesses distinguish their digital experiences in ways that make it extremely challenging for Amazon to compete with them.

In our experience, B2B customers want to be overwhelmed in a different way. Here's what B2B customers want.

Not Just Sales; Useful Information

How many times have you gone to YouTube to check out a video when your dishwasher floods or some other appliance malfunctions? Great B2B manufacturers ensure that their digital property is the world's best source for research about their product and the problems it was intended to solve. In the middle of the COVID-19 outbreak, 3M released its COVID-19 resources center, where it included guides for cleaning and disinfecting respirators and respirator training videos. While that information may have been available elsewhere, the 3M digital team clearly decided that the company needed to be an authority not just on its products but also on the use of its products. At Bloomreach, we offered our own COVID-19 research center, providing weekly data on the e-commerce trend lines across geographies and industries. The goal was not just to sell our products but also to have our brand become synonymous with the category—all while being helpful. That data generated some of the largest website interest we have ever seen, proving that building for research isn't just about brand awareness; it's also about B2B lead generation. Replicating deep research on a topic is hard for a marketplace-oriented vendor like Amazon that lacks the deep domain expertise and feedback loops that make quality research destinations stand out.

Not Just Products; Services, Solutions, and Tools

Winning digital experiences in B2B are centered on providing solutions and tools, not just products. HD Supply accompanies its property management products with renovation and installation services. Upon scheduling a consultation online and receiving a quote, a dedicated renovations manager will facilitate everything from project management to product advice, forecasting, volume discounts, and even labor in selected areas. Expertise sells. The Carrier Enterprise brand Watsco takes the idea of advice to a whole new level. Watsco has completely transformed its relationship with its customers via digital. Core to the strategy has been a series of digital customer success tools, all designed to deepen relationships with day-to-day users of Watsco's HVAC systems. A visit to carrierenterprise.com will showcase a range of time-saving tools, including a part-finder tool to help repairpersons easily find parts, an AHRI system builder for HVAC systems to allow a dealer or contractor to configure a system that can be easily matched and certified, and a document finder to help technicians come to one place to access all documents needed for installation and service work. Those three tools are just the beginning. There are digital business productivity tools to provide fast access to a range of business processes. There is a mobile app to help contractors on the job stock warehouses and truck inventory and handle express pickup. There are even tools to help contractors sell to and service their customers, including everything from quote builders to sale trackers to house-call streamliners. So why would an HVAC supplier get into the software business to build such an incredible assortment of digital tools? Because every one of the digital interactions makes the customer more and more sticky to the products and services being offered by the Watsco brands. Think Amazon can replicate that for the HVAC space? Unlikely.

Not Serendipity; Familiarity

While the B2C consumer may be delighted by the experience of shopping and finding something new and surprising, B2B users hate all that. Surprises are definitely not a good thing, and "serendipity" is just another way of saying "took me an hour of clicking around to find what I wanted." That hour costs money. The B2B customer comes to the digital experience in search of speed and ease of use. Indeed, a B2B experience needs to feel a lot more like a grocery list than a fashion wish list. Nowhere is the power of familiarity more clear than in one of the greatest B2B businesses of all—Salesforce. Salesforce is a gold standard in B2B software. Its interfaces and the constructs we as users have gotten used to are seared in our brains. The customer relationship

Figure 9.2 HD Supply ensures the B2B experience is as good as a B2C experience. Shutterstock.

management (CRM) system that Salesforce pioneered in the cloud has now been adopted by over 150,000 organizations with anywhere from tens to thousands of employees. And while Salesforce aims to be innovative, it has a large installed base that expects familiarity. So when Salesforce launched its mobile app, no one expected a host of new concepts. Log in to the Salesforce mobile app, as I do often, and you will see largely the same basic navigation structure that you find on the web-based interface. You'll see accounts, opportunities, contacts, leads, dashboards, and reports, followed by a range of other less-frequented tabs. Most of those basic concepts haven't changed in years. Indeed, so many challengers have questioned whether these are the right concepts for a modern CRM system—offering other, sometimes better alternatives. But B2B users like familiarity. I'm looking to get in and out of Salesforce and know what the outlook for my business is. Familiarity is often the best answer.

Not Just Efficiency; Trust

This may seem counterintuitive. Of course, every business craves efficiency, and Amazon is the king of frictionless commerce. Indeed, a study by McKinsey found that B2B customers vastly prefer self-service to directed sales in every step of the sales process—a clear plea for efficiency. But there is something a business customer will trade even efficiency for, and that's trust. Businesses want to save time and money—but only when that results in a positive outcome. A money-saving move that fails to solve the business problem is a disaster. If you order shoes that are a great buy but end up having cheap soles that wear through, that's a bummer but hardly a tragedy. If instead of shoes you order personal protective equipment for a hospital and it wears through unexpectedly, that's a very different conversation. The time and money savings are not just a waste; they're the reason you lose your job . . . or your company goes under . . . or there's a lawsuit resulting from the defective items you purchased. Efficiency is a good thing, but trust is paramount. B2B users will put up with a lot if they trust the result. The digital experience must reflect that priority.

How might trust manifest in a B2B digital experience? Often it starts with the people. Sales, service, and account managers have been the backbone of B2B businesses for a long time. And for most high-quality salespeople, disappointing a trusted client has the dual effect of losing a customer for the business and burning a relationship for their career. The best digital experiences empower those salespeople with excellent tools to help them add more and more value for their clients. The days of long, wine-filled lunches and golf boondoggles are behind us. To gain the trust of the customer, salespeople need to bring knowledge, value, and expertise to the table. The digital team can help. That might mean providing alerts on the health or activities of the account, information on how effective the solution is in driving business outcomes, digital previews of new capabilities and products, and competitive information presented to equip the salesperson for success. Most B2B software businesses have entire functions dedicated to sales enablement and customer success, often manifesting in a digital drip feed of important information, training, and assets, intended to make sure their salespeople are smarter than their competitors' salespeople. It's essential for the B2B digital team to understand that digitally enabling the company's other teams is a key way to cement competitive advantage, and for them to treat the salesperson as a proxy for the customer.

OPTIMIZE FOR B2B METRICS

No discussion of winning digital experiences can be complete without a careful examination of the key operational and financial metrics that represent B2B success. While many of the classic digital metrics—monthly active users, engagement, conversion rates, bounce rates, and others—may apply, B2B businesses have come to understand that they need to optimize for different and equally important goals. Let's start with the user or seeker journey.

Many, though not all, B2C experiences tend to be transactional in nature. You visit an app or a website seeking a product or solution and ultimately select what you are looking for. You will likely either save that product in the cart to buy it later or complete the transaction in a single session. You will certainly consider alternatives on other digital properties or Google or Amazon. In B2B, visits to digital properties can have significantly different purposes. The research engineer may be studying solutions, the maintenance person may be checking order status, and the procurement person may be reordering. They may all belong to the same customer—they're just different heads of the monster. But together they represent the voice of the customer. Treating each of these personas independently can create a high-quality experience, but it all comes together in the form of the lifetime value (LTV) of the customer. LTV metrics aim to capture the long-term value of the customer. They capture the design wins and the transactional business. They capture today's purchases but also track the growth, decline, and even churn of an account over time. The LTV calculation divides the average revenue you earn from an account over a given time period by the percentage of customers that leave you over that same time period. A more advanced version considers the margin on that customer. An LTV of 3 means that your average customer stays with you for three years. The higher the lifetime value is, the more you can invest to acquire and retain that customer.

So why does this all matter? It matters because every major initiative in B2B should be evaluated against the transaction and in-session metrics like conversion rate and revenue per visit and also against the LTV. A winning digital experience extends LTV either by reducing churn or by driving account growth, and it does all that by transferring mundane tasks from people to the digital experience.

EMBRACE THE MULTIHEADED SEEKER

In so many ways, the characteristics of winning digital experiences— that they are built for the seeker, that they are built on a digital experience platform, and that they are built by digitally native product-centric organizations—are the same across B2B and B2C. Taming the multiheaded monster of B2B may look daunting at first, but it is fundamentally about applying those winning principles and then adjusting strategies to deliver winning experiences to each head. The narrative that B2B simply needs to catch up with B2C is wrong. B2B experiences are unique, and competing with Amazon and winning is entirely possible as long as the game is being played on the right field. It means personalizing across the right dimensions, prioritizing efficiency and accuracy, learning from the offline world, building for the research needs of complex decisions, extending from products to services and tools, valuing familiarity, and optimizing for the right metrics.

Once the monster has been tamed, the road to winning becomes clear. We are entering a golden age of B2B digital disruption.

10

MAX OUT THE R_0

We learned far too much about viruses and their spread in 2020. COVID-19, it turns out, is particularly deadly because it has a high mortality rate and a high infection rate. That infection rate, scientifically termed the R_0, represents the rate at which the virus can spread. COVID-19's R_0 is estimated to be 2.2–2.7. That means at least 80 percent of the population needs to be immune in order to avoid spread, assuming an incubation period of 4.2 days and a disease doubling time of 2–3 days.

But the virus isn't the only thing that spread quickly that year. As we locked down and masked up, efforts to move to a 100 percent digital business became more urgent.

At Bloomreach, we saw that very clearly. Our application programming interface (API) call volume, reflecting the demand on the largest e-commerce and digital brands on the planet, skyrocketed, up 85 percent year-over-year. Our average customer saw 50 percent growth in its e-commerce business, with certain categories like groceries up over 500 percent. We were in a completely different age of digital after just a few months. If retail e-commerce accounted for 16 percent of total retail prepandemic, even after stores were reopening, it was hitting 30 percent. After growing 15 percent year-over-year for so many years, e-commerce adoption almost doubled in a few months—accelerating the R_0 of digital by almost five years.

That speed poses a new question to business: Are you ready?

If digital transformation was a goal pre-COVID-19, in the postvirus world it's an imperative. The patterns that consumers and businesses experienced in the pandemic are largely here to stay. While certainly some of that spending has started to revert to stores, we can expect more home haircuts than ever before. We can expect segments of the population that never leaned on digital (for example, older consumers) to fall in love with it. We can expect laggard digital categories (like groceries) to accelerate quickly. And we can expect consumers to spend a much larger fraction of their discretionary income digitally.

Bloomreach's research confirms that 40 percent of consumers and 56 percent of buyers would pay more for a better experience. That's the good news. On the other hand, 80 percent of those same respondents confirm that they would abandon digital experiences where the basics are not in place. What are the basics? Easy-to-find products, attractive websites and apps, simple shipping policies, well-laid-out product information, and a personalized experience. While online demand has skyrocketed, many businesses that are reliant on offline investments are rapidly shifting their budgets. Our survey confirmed that investment in offline has been cut in half, while 60 percent of respondents plan to increase investment in digital and online activities. Equally interesting is where companies planned to invest in digital. While 64 percent plan to increase investments in the digital customer experience, the smallest beneficiary of digital budgets is omnichannel, which enables digital in physical locations. Instead, 52 percent plan to invest in virtual reality, augmented reality, or 3D technology. Indeed, everyone is looking to become a digital native.

None of these trends are new, but the pace, the R_0, has accelerated. The stakes for digital have never been higher, and the opportunity has never been more compelling. With boards and senior executives scrambling to respond, the question for all digital teams is the same: How do you max out the R_0 of digital?

THE WINNER'S CHECKLIST

How can organizations know where they stand in terms of digital preparedness? Having been through the earlier chapters, you are well versed on what it takes to win. The question now becomes, How ready are you? The following ten-point checklists cover the three major areas that winners conquer.

SECTION 1: SEEKER CENTRICITY

1. Is digital thought of as a line of business, not a channel for you?
2. Can you identify the *why* behind what your customer buys from you?
3. Do you know who your seeker is?
4. Does your digital team know who your seeker is?
5. Does everyone in your company know who your seeker is?
6. Is your core offering built for the seeker?
7. Is your digital offering differentiated enough that the seeker cannot go out and find a largely equivalent alternative?
8. Do you use data signals to tune your offering?
9. Does your digital offering automatically get better as you sleep at night?
10. Do you deliver a highly personalized experience to each one of your seekers?

If you answered yes to ten out of these ten questions, you have fully reinvented your business around the seeker and set yourself up for long-term digital nirvana. If you're at five, you're midway through your journey. If you're at one, you're on the verge of being disrupted by someone who has reimagined your customer as a seeker.

SECTION 2: BUILD ON A DIGITAL EXPERIENCE PLATFORM

1. Can you give an example of where you use ambient interfaces (wearables, internet of things, mobile devices) to collect data that you use in your digital experience?

2. Do you use artificial intelligence (AI) in your digital experience to automate or solve a problem that could be solved at scale only by a machine?

3. Is your technology stack API based?

4. If a business user wants to make a simple content or user experience change on your website or app, can they do it in minutes?

5. If a developer wants to connect to a new data source or integrate a new functional capability on your website or app, can they do it in weeks?

6. Do you have a digital experience platform that is the basis for building new experiences?

7. Do you do releases at least once every two weeks?

8. Could your system scale to at least two times the average load you see and survive a major cloud provider going down?

9. Is your information security person or team integrated into your digital team?

10. Do you understand how the AI makes decisions?

A modern technology stack is a competitive weapon. Businesses that don't have one can have the best vision of a compelling digital experience that is seeker centric and still fail because they simply cannot keep up with the innovation velocity of their competitors. The Web is a hypercompetitive place, and so many companies tell the tale of an inflexible platform gating progress. Winners understand that technology is a core competency, not a cost center, and give it the same care, feeding, and investment as their crown jewels. Same deal on the platform checklist. If you're at one or two yeses, you're really at the starting gate. If you're at nine or ten, you're set.

SECTION 3: BUILD WITH A PRODUCT-CENTRIC DIGITAL TEAM

1. Do you have a clearly defined digital team?

2. Does the digital team have responsibility for more than e-commerce, including the digital transformation of your core business?

3. Do you have a digital leader who is a digital native?

4. Have you failed more than one time at digital?

5. Do you have a product management team dedicated to digital?

6. Do you have people responsible for all the other key digital competencies: development, data science, digital marketing, design, digital merchandising, and (in business-to-business settings) sales?
7. Does your digital offering have an outcome-driven business model—transactional, subscription, or consumption?
8. Is your marketing organization focused across channels rather than being channel specific?
9. Do you have a flywheel strategy—that is, some form of digital network effect driven by building a platform, enrolling an ecosystem, or building a digital marketplace?
10. Do you measure against short- and longer-term goals (like lifetime value of the customer)?

Winning organizations have winning digital teams that are the heartbeat driving both transformation and near-term results. The quality of talent on those teams ultimately determines the organization's destiny. But equally important is how those teams are set up: whether the business model and practices support their success, whether the culture is adaptable to change, and whether there is a willingness to embrace different business models and tolerate risk can be the difference between talented people who succeed and those who walk out the door frustrated. The baseline for good in a winning team is higher than in the other categories. Five out of ten yeses means you are really at the starting gate.

But in what order should businesses and organizations address the three major areas of focus: reinventing the customer, building the technology platform, and building the team? Of course, there is recursive iteration in these steps. Often I see organizations start with the team. The theory is that with the right people, anything can happen. In a start-up, that is true. But larger and older organizations that have a history of success outside digital have much more to contend with than simply recruiting talent. In fact, they are much more likely to pay lip service to digital, declaring that it is the centerpiece of a future strategy to Wall Street and at all company meetings and then not backing it up with the hard changes it takes to win.

Too often organizations will start with talent or technology. It's an understandable error. Boards and consultants will argue that without the right talent or technology, nothing else matters. They will then go off and try to recruit the best Silicon Valley team—or worse, they will set up an outpost in Silicon Valley to attract talent in the most competitive labor market in the world. Third-rate engineers will join, they will be left outside the halls of power, and digital will go nowhere.

That's why I believe it actually makes the most sense to focus first on reinventing the customer around a seeker. If leadership can converge around who the seeker *really* is and what it takes to win them, the rest becomes a lot easier—because almost every organization is centered around the person paying the bills, often a user or customer. Driving alignment around a reimagined view of that individual or business will force leadership to rethink everything from the offering to the business model to the marketing. Once there is alignment around that, it is time to bring in the team and empower its members to be product centric and define the digital strategy. Step three is then the technology. Only with a clear definition of the problem and a technology-knowledgeable team can the right platform be selected and innovated on. Swapping the customer for the seeker is the essential first step on the path to winning. It's important to start with the heart of the business, the customer, and reinvent who the business can be built for. That in turn will form the basis to attract world-class talent, and the stakes will be too high to put them in a far-off outpost. That talent will then know exactly how to use the tools of the trade to invest in the kind of technology innovation that creates winners.

BUYING YOUR WAY TO NIRVANA

Following the winner's playbook is hard work. Change doesn't come easy, so it is no accident that so many try to accelerate the transformation with acquisitions. Acquisitions can absolutely work as a means to getting to a winning digital result. The story of Walmart .com is such a success story. In April 2011, Walmart, watching e-commerce take off, bought Kosmix, a nascent technology company based in Silicon Valley, for $300 million. It marketed the acquisition as the creation of "Walmart Labs." While the technology was interesting, it was mostly about talent. Venky Hariharan and Anand Rajaraman were early e-commerce pioneers; their first business, Junglee, was previously acquired by Amazon. The Walmart Labs team did make an impact, modernizing Walmart's e-commerce stack and teaching the company what it meant to build a true digital division. Over time, as many of the best people left, Walmart started to lag. While Walmart.com was valuable, it was still a small offshoot of the mothership, hardly consequential to the behemoth retail establishment. Slowly but surely Walmart.com was being outpaced by Amazon and so many digital rivals. But Walmart didn't stop being aggressive. In 2016, it spent $3 billion to buy Jet.com, the price-optimized marketplace started by another digital stalwart, Mark Lore. Mark has led Walmart's e-commerce business since then. In 2020, Walmart wound down Jet.com, inviting criticism that its acquisition was pricey and a waste of money. Nothing could be further from the truth than that. Between 2017 and 2019, Walmart saw a 207 percent increase in its e-commerce buyer base and became the technology innovator no one expected—recently releasing its own version of Amazon Prime, building a strong marketplace, and even experimenting with innovative services like automatically stocking a refrigerator based on alerts. Walmart's stock in the last four years has almost doubled. Not quite Amazon's stock performance, but nothing to sneeze at and a great return on $3 billion.

So why did Walmart's bets in mergers and acquisitions pay off when so many others have failed. To put it simply, it was willing to bet big. So many boards and management teams tinker with digital, bringing in those with "digital DNA" and setting them up in a small silo of the organization. That simply doesn't work. Transformations don't happen by giving the change agents a small part in the movie. The change agents need to have the lead roles.

LOOKING AHEAD: THE NEXT GENERATION OF WINNERS

We know who won big in the first two decades of digital—FAANG: Facebook, Amazon, Apple, Netflix, and Google. Their stories have been well chronicled, and as of April 2020, they represent 12 percent of the S&P 500. Microsoft is not always included in the group, but it has certainly had a cloud-based renaissance. These businesses have been accompanied by BAT: the Chinese internet giants Baidu, Alibaba, and Tencent.

What's been true of all these companies? They have provided highly scalable, horizontal digital utilities for millions and millions of people. In the case of Facebook, it's been social networking. For Amazon, it's been shopping. For Apple, it's been computing. For Netflix, it's been content and media. And for Google, it's been search. The analogy to the telecommunications, utility, and railroad oligopolies is a good one. But a century later very few people remember the Union Pacific Railroad, once the dominant player in the railroad industry.

That's because change looks like it's never going to come, and then it comes really quickly when the moment is right. Now is one of those moments.

Political actors across the world are eying the tech monopolies. Regulators are beating records in terms of fines and antitrust investigations. The brand perceptions of many of these businesses are suffering. And consumers, while still invested in the big internet companies, are starting to realize that there are other games in town.

So who wins the next twenty years?

If the last twenty years have been about laying down the tracks and building the railroads, the next twenty years are going to be about the incredible businesses and organizations that will be built to take advantage of the infrastructure that FAANG and its global counterparts have built.

As more and more activities shift to being digital-first, the winners will be those who start to build the killer apps. The task at hand is not to beat Amazon or Google. It is to win the digital race in your specific vertical or line of business. It is to be the world's best digital bank or, better yet, the world's best store of money. It is to be the world's best digital hospital or, better yet, the world's best digital caregiving service. What's great about these opportunities is that they need deep, industry-specific expertise. A smart group of Silicon Valley engineers will struggle to understand the nuances of the health care system and the banking system, both much different problems than social networking or web search. They will certainly try. But the contenders can equally come from current banks or current hospitals. The good news is that banks and hospitals no longer need to invent the plumbing. Strong engineers are being trained by technology companies everywhere. Capital is abundant. Cloud infrastructure is available by the drink. Customers and consumers are hungry to work with brands they trust and are always willing to try new services. They will benefit from a seamless interplay between physical commerce or service and digital commerce or service. The next twenty years will be won by highly specialized, vertical digital experiences that take hundreds of years of domain experience and translate them to uniquely satisfy the seeker, all while leveraging the unfair advantages that these businesses have—knowledge, relationships, brand affinity, distribution, capital, and so many others.

We see contenders everywhere. Sure, Tesla, a car company no one had heard of ten years ago, is the leader in electric cars. But after Tesla's Model 3 and Model S come the Chevy Volt and the Nissan Leaf. Chevrolet and Nissan were hardly viewed as the world's most innovative companies, but they are contenders. All kinds of start-ups invested in wearables and connected clothing for athletes. But great athletic apparel brands like Nike, Adidas, and Bloomreach customer Puma have continued to set the digital innovation pace. So many others will seize the opportunity to lap the competition and build winning digital experiences in their specific digital race.

MISSION IS THE NEW MAGIC

Following the winner's playbook will get you to the promised land. But occasionally you will find a digital experience that doesn't just win—it seems to be magical. Those digital experiences are the virtual world's equivalent of a child arriving for the first time at Disneyland and being transported to the faraway lands of fairy tales and fragrant sugar-filled churros. What is that magic in digital?

The world is increasingly driven by millennials and Gen Zers who do not want to do business the old-fashioned way. The members of the Depression Generation were frugal for life. Those in the COVID-19 Generation will be similarly marked by their experience. They're looking for mission and meaning in everything. They want to believe deeply in their jobs, their favorite brands, and their careers. They want meaning. They want mission.

Indeed, mission is the new magic.

Great digital experiences will certainly win by satisfying the seeker. But it turns out that the millennial seeker wants the chosen products and services to represent their values. It used to be that business and civic or political engagement lived in totally separate spheres of life. You worked with people who might have differing views and served customers who likely had a wide assortment of political and philosophical persuasions. The norms were straightforward—stay out of politically charged, identity-oriented topics. But the combination of seeking missions and living one's work and personal lives online has fused everything. It has then been turbocharged with polarized politics.

So what does any of this have to do with winning experiences?

It means that some of the truly unique experiences appeal not just to the seeker's motivations to solve a problem or achieve an outcome but also to the seeker's sensibilities. It means that those experiences are built by digital teams that do more than put the product first; they believe deeply in the mission statement of the experiences they are pouring their life into. Let's look at Impossible Brands. Impossible was started in 2009 by a Stanford professor, Patrick Brown, who switched career directions to urgently make a dent in climate change. He wanted to make the global food system, a huge contributor to carbon emissions, sustainable by making meat, fish, and dairy from plants. Impossible describes its mission as "to restore biodiversity and reduce the impact of climate change by transforming the global food system. To do this we make delicious, nutritious, affordable and sustainable meat, fish and dairy from plants." Enter the Impossible Burger—which tastes as delicious as any burger but is sourced from plants. It is first and foremost a scientific breakthrough. But at its core, it is a true reimagination of the customer as seeker. Meat substitutes have existed for a long time. And environmentalists and healthy-eating advocates have pushed vegetarianism for a long time. Impossible's insight is that many people like meat, and that isn't going to change. But saving the earth from climate change is certainly a mission that many can get behind.

What if meat could be synthetically created from plants to taste just as good and, if adopted widely, could move the needle on climate change? Impossible doesn't aim to convert meat eaters to vegetarians; it aims to create sustainable meat.

The Impossible digital experience tugs at all the same sensibilities and conveys the same mission. It is a classic direct-to-consumer brand that has many of the same challenges that new brands often have. Where does it get distribution? Impossible understands that there is a strong relationship between the ability to attract distribution—restaurants, grocery stores, and other food distributors—and the visibility of its consumer brand. In a predigital world, the company might have done what many other food brands do: advertise on TV, hire salespeople to sign up distribution channels, and look to take market share. But digital allows it to extend its brand and its reach. It is now present in thousands of coffee shops, grocery stores, and restaurants. How did that happen so quickly? No doubt because the innovation was powerful, but its digital experience certainly played a key role.

The Impossible website presents beautiful imagery that conveys how tasty its food is. It includes a number of tasty recipes, understanding that its seeker needs to be inspired to cook with its sustainable meat products—without that, evangelizing Impossible will be hard. The digital property also understands that there are many different personas that need to be served—including restaurant owners (business-to-business) and consumers (business-to-consumer). It is a logged-in experience that, like Stitch Fix or Peloton, asks a number of questions about preferences (in this case, about food rather than fashion or fitness). It allows for personalization by creating a "My Recipes" section. It includes a point system that ultimately drives loyalty. Clearly Impossible is setting the stage for what could ultimately be more than a one-time purchase, perhaps leading to other business models.

But in addition to all the digital best practices, Impossible has a secret weapon—its mission. The mission is presented digitally front and center—articulating that the product needs "less land, less water and less greenhouse gases." Certainly in doing this, there will be some who, because of personal or political preference, will shy away from Impossible. At a time when brand success was overwhelmingly driven by risk-averse retail distribution channels, downplaying the mission might have been the right call. But digital has changed everything. Impossible has even launched a direct-to-commerce site—you can buy its products directly from its website. Which meat-product vendor ever did that predigital? Since digital is by definition a global channel with incredible reach, standing out from the crowd with mission pays off because you find consumers and business who share your vision and subscribe or purchase with high conviction. The company has clearly decided that putting mission front and center is both the right thing to do and good business.

Impossible is not alone in its category. Its key rival is Beyond Meat, which is an equally innovative company. But watch any interview with the CEO of Impossible, and when asked about Beyond, he will wish them well. He doesn't view Beyond as his competition; rather, the much larger meat industry is his competition. Employees will be proud of that decision. Investors will double down. And seekers will buy not just because it's a great offering but also because it's consistent with their value system. Impossible may not have the capital or the customers or the distribution of the multibillion-dollar incumbent in its space, JBS, the Brazilian meat giant. And certainly JBS understands that sustainability in food is important, even including a section of its website that says "JBS feeds millions of people around the world, and we are committed to doing so as sustainably as possible." But it then goes on to market its core products in beef, chicken, and pork. In one case, sustainability feels like something a marketing team has added to a website. In the other case, the entire offering seems centered on the seeker's desire to eat tasty sustainable meats.

Watch out, JBS. Mission sells. And in digital, mission *really* sells.

THE HAPPINESS BOOM

Where will all this leave us postpandemic? Here's the good news for humanity: as we move beyond the virus, digital has set us up for two booms—an economic boom and a much more profound happiness boom. The digital acceleration we have seen because of COVID-19

Figure 10.1 Digital has set us up for an economic boom and a more profound happiness boom. Shutterstock.

has and will continue to transform our economy at hyperspeed, and it will usher in an economic boom equal in magnitude to the one we saw in the first twenty years of the twenty-first century, postinternet. We will see an incredible productivity increase because more and more businesses will shift from an 80–20 physical-to-virtual ratio to a 20–80 ratio in favor of virtual. They'll do it because they are much more productive that way. Employees who commute will gain two hours back every day. Costs will also drop, as employees will travel only when they must and businesses will reduce their spending on corporate real estate and be able to hire in any location where they can find talent. Innovation will also soar. Much as we saw when Google and online advertising took off as a lower-cost, higher-return marketing channel after the recession in 2001–2003 and when Airbnb and Uber rose after the 2008 economic crisis, the current economic challenges will usher in a new wave of innovators. We will see self-sanitizing doorknobs or face recognition and voice interaction systems that avoid the need for touchscreens or digital health-tracing applications. Some of the innovation will work, and others will fail—but a lot will change.

The really good news is that accompanying the economic boom will be a new kind of happiness boom. We will do the things we have to do digitally and do more of the things we want to do physically. Those with increasingly digital jobs won't have to go to work. Those who don't enjoy it won't have to go to the grocery store or the bank. But if we don't have to commute to the office or run errands physically, we'll be even more interested in family vacations in other cities or countries. We'll go to bars and restaurants with friends more often. We'll play more sports and go for more hikes in parks. Because while digital is amazing in all the things it can do to improve productivity, COVID-19 has also taught us that we really miss each other and that no Zoom call or website interaction replaces a night out with friends or a family gathering.

As more and more digital teams create winning digital experiences, we all win. The team members win and rise in their careers. Businesses win by driving a new era of digital growth. Consumers win by getting more time back and achieving more and more of their goals online. Happiness abounds.

But the digital happiness opportunity doesn't stop there. If we do this right, all of humanity has the opportunity to win big because digital can be the great equalizer. We know that the economic boom of the last several decades has created incredible amounts of success—but also incredible amounts of inequality. We know that in the United States, white families have twenty times the wealth of black families. We have seen essential workers who have been on the front lines fighting COVID-19 for the rest of us bear the brunt of the sacrifice and the disproportionate impact the disease has had on low-income communities. And we know that deep poverty, lack of health care, lack of education, and lack of opportunity pervade much of the world. So what can digital do about all of this? It can be the great equalizer.

For the first time in human history, it is actually possible to create great digital experiences that solve the great problems of our time—for everyone. We can start with education. Building on the success of my friend Sal Khan, who started Khan Academy, we can build the kind of winning, highly personalized digital education experience that extends from early education through higher education—all without needing expensive university systems funded by crushing student debt. We can build a world-class digital health care experience. Prat Vemana, chief digital officer of Kaiser Permanente, talks publicly about how telemedicine grew fifteenfold during the COVID-19 lockdown. The best medical care didn't shut down. It became accessible to many more people—on demand. No doubt digital pioneers like Sal and Prat will tell us that we have a long way to go to really achieve the dreams of great digital education or health care. But what if we could deliver good education or health care digitally to seven billion people worldwide. Wouldn't that be better than delivering great education or health care to a few?

Digital makes that all possible. And that's when we all really win.

ACKNOWLEDGMENTS

Writing a book has always been on my bucket list. For that, I want to thank my father, Surajit De Datta, who always believed in research, knowledge, and scholarship. His writings, including his book *Principles and Practices of Rice Production*, have left a lasting imprint on me. I want to thank my mother, Vijji De Datta, whose insatiable curiosity to learn—anything and anytime—leaves me breathless with admiration.

A number of friends and professional acquaintances who have written books also motivated me, including Charles Duhigg, Nick Mehta, Sal Khan, Jeff Norton, and Hemant Taneja. Thank you for all of your advice along the way.

This book could not have happened without so many current and former Bloomreachers; many of their insights form the basis for my writing. Christy Augustine, Will Uppington, Amit Aggarwal, Srinath Sridhar, Xun Wang, Albert Wang, Luis Sala, Ross Williams, Brian Walker, Rob Rosenthal, Dave Pomeroy, Arje Cahn, Samit Paul, and Ravi Raj—thank you. A special thanks to Ajay Agarwal from Bain Capital Ventures, who wrote a $5 million check to help us start Bloomreach over ten years ago and set us on a path to build a great company for the digital seeker. Peter Nieh, Ravi Viswanathan, Hilarie Koplow-McAdams, and Marcus Ryu have been incredible members of our board of directors. Thank you for picking me up in the tough times and inspiring me to be a better leader always.

The Digital Seeker is really not my story or Bloomreach's story; it is the story of transformative leaders who show us the path to a new age of digital. I want to thank David Frankel, Micah Rosenbloom, and Eric Paley for their insights around disruptive start-ups, their friendship, and their stewardship of Founder Collective. It's been a pleasure to serve with Martin Blackman on the Council of Champions at the United States Tennis Association. Martin, thank you for sharing your transformative story of artificial intelligence and analytics in tennis. Thank you to technology and business luminaries George Mathew, Faisal Masud, Julie Bornstein, Tim Walters, Robert Chatwani, Sam Shank, Alex Rampell, and Joseph Pine. Each of them is an expert in their respective field and contributed significantly to my thinking. I've learned from so many of our customers who gave me their time, including Steve Baruch at MSC Industrial, Benjamin Stoll at FIFA, Roger Donald at NHS Digital, Brooke Logan at HD Supply, John Strain at Gap Inc., John Koryl at Canadian Tire, Christina Callas at Total Wine, Jim Denny at Cedar Fair, Salee Suwansawad at Old Navy, and Sameer Hassan at Williams-Sonoma. They, along with all our other customers and partners, are the true heroes of this book, masters of their digital craft.

This book was really jointly written with Ellen Neuborne. Without her expertise in business writing, commitment to keeping me on track, and unrelenting positivity, a book like this would not have been possible. Thank you as well to my literary agents, Greg Shaw and James Levine, who shepherded the book through a publishing landscape that was totally new to me. Thank you to Ben Kolstad and his team at KnowledgeWorks Global for their editorial support. And special thanks to Myles Thompson and his team at Columbia Business School Publishing, who made a bet that we could introduce the business world to the concept of the digital seeker.

Finally, I want to thank my wonderful wife and kids, who afforded me the time, space, and joyous energy of a loving family to complete this book. Riya and Surya, thanks for being unquenchable learners and making me laugh every day. Sangeeta, thanks for twenty years of love, support, and being "all in" on building a life together.

INDEX

Page numbers in *italics* indicate figures or tables.